Yossel Rakover Speaks to God

Holocaust Challenges to Religious Faith

Zvi Kolitz

Yossel Rakover Speaks to God

Holocaust Challenges to Religious Faith

Zvi Kolitz

KTAV Publishing House, Inc,
Hoboken, New Jersey

Library of Congress Cataloging-in-Publication Data

Kolitz, Zvi
    Yossel Rakover speaks to God : Holocaust challenges to religious faith /
Zvi Kolitz
        p.   cm.
        ISBN 0-88125-526-2 : $19.95
        1. Holocaust (Jewish theology) I. Title
    BM645.H6K65   1995
    296.3—dc20   95–18831
                                                                          CIP

Manufactured in the United States of America
KTAV Publishing House, 900 Jefferson Street, Hoboken NJ, 07030

To Sarah Korein
A dear friend
A great lady
A woman of valor

Contents

✣

Foreword

᛭

Norman Lamm

The context of Zvi Kolitz's "Yossel Rakover Speaks to God" is one of the most frightful in all of history, one of despair and defiance, defeat and triumph. The time is April, 1943, in the midst of World War II. The scene is Warsaw, in one of the few houses that remained standing as the Jewish ghetto was about to go up in flames, for the Nazi Wehrmacht was bringing in heavy artillery to put down the revolt by a handful of impoverished, starving, diseased, poorly armed but determined Jewish survivors. The document purports to be a statement by one Yossel Rakover, a Polish Hasidic Jew, who pens this incredible testament as he awaits certain death.

All of this is, of course, a "story" by Zvi Kolitz, an Israeli Jew of distinguished Lithuanian ancestry, who lives in New York and is a journalist, producer, essayist, thinker, and a teacher at Yeshiva University. His relation to his creation is itself an interesting story. So powerful is the verisimilitude of his account that it was taken as a bona fide document salvaged from the ruins of the ghetto,

Norman Lamm is President and Jakob and Erna Michael Professor of Jewish Philosophy at Yeshiva University, New York and as a result the work assumed a life of its own. In actuality, it was written by Zvi Kolitz in Yiddish and published in 1946 in a Yiddish newspaper in Buenos Aires, where he was visiting on behalf of the Zionist Revisionist movement. An anonymous reader of the story presented it to *Di Goldene Keyt* in Israel as a text discovered in the rubble of the Warsaw ghetto. Edited by the poet Abraham Sutzkever, a survivor of the Vilna ghetto, the story appeared in Israel in Yiddish and was then published in French translation in 1955. The French version was read by the distinguished Franco-Jewish philosopher Emmanuel Levinas and occasioned his essay reprinted in this volume. A Hebrew version appeared in Israel in 1965. None of these versions mentions the author, Zvi Kolitz.

Indeed, as the Kabbalah taught, "everything depends upon luck, even the Scroll of the Torah in the Ark" (Zohar III, 134a). Zvi Kolitz's literary device of using the pseudonymous Yossel Rakover as his spokesman almost succeeded in obliterating his own authorship, but ultimately "luck" smiled upon him, and his name will always be attached to this truly precious gem.

"Yossel Rakover" is one of the most inspired writings to emerge from the vast and growing body of literature on the Holocaust. It is not "history." It is not, strictly speaking, theology. It is not poetry. It is not even fiction—hence the remarkable amnesia that erased the real author's name and assumed that the testament and the story of its provenance were factual, rather than a brilliant literary construction by an inspired writer-thinker-feeler who had transmuted his deepest and mightiest reactions to the most horrendous cataclysm in centuries into a contemporary myth, i.e., a truth far beyond mere facticity.

But if it is neither history nor theology nor fiction, what is it?

"Yossel Rakover" is the wrenching meditation of a naked, tormented soul that refuses to surrender its innate dignity; a deeply gripping spiritual address to his Creator by a believing Jew who, in his indescribable suffering, is not ready to yield either his faith or his rationality, and who speaks as a profoundly Jewish Jew. Like Jacob of old, "the choicest of the forefathers," he "strived with God and men, and he prevailed" (Gen. 32:29). Kolitz's Yossel Rakover wrestles with his God, but unlike the protagonists of some of the literary works that have emerged from the Holocaust, he does not "put God in the dock" and presume to judge Him. Such fictional "trials" can be and sometimes are serious dialogues that commend themselves to readers who, though far removed from the searing experience of the Holocaust both in time and in biography, seek a genuine encounter, even confrontation, with God; one can trace the history of such defiant challenges to Abraham's pleading for Sodom and to Job, and much later to the Hasidic accounts of Rabbi Levi Yitzchak of Berdichev. But they run the risk of becoming quite maudlin and cheap, plucking at the heartstrings of the victims in a manner that is spiritually unauthentic; the mock "trial" becomes an exercise in barely disguised atheism, exploiting the suffering of the protagonists as a way of denying rather than engaging God.

"Yossel Rakover" is nothing of the sort. It is at once subtle and direct, and constitutes a truly religious encounter because Yossel Rakover never questions the existence of a Creator. Instead, he defiantly declares, in words borrowed from a great medieval story of suffering and faith, that he will believe no matter how much God pushes him into disbelief. And his meditation goes beyond the kind of catharsis that results from the justifiable but not necessarily enlightening dramatic tension of a trial with God as the accused.

A central theme of "Yossel Rakover" is *hester panim*—the "hiding of God's face" or "veiling of God's countenance," two English renderings of the biblical idiom in Deuteronomy 31:17–18:

> Then My anger shall be kindled against them in that day, and I will forsake them, and I will hide My face from them, and they shall be devoured, and many evils and troubles shall come upon them, so that they will say in that day, "Are not these evils come upon us because our God is not among us?" And I will surely hide My face in that day for all the evil which they have wrought, in that they are turned to other gods.

Professor Levinas expands on this theme in his essay in this book, but there is much more that has been said and that remains to be said about it. Without ever mentioning the term, the sages of the Talmud read the concept of *hester panim* into the Song of Moses, slightly changing the verse "Who is like unto Thee amongst the mighty (*ba-elim*), O Lord?" (Exod. 15:11) to read, "Who is like unto thee amongst the silent (*ba-ilmim*), O Lord?" This was a remarkable anticipation of the anonymous inscription on the wall of a cellar in Cologne where Jews hid themselves throughout the Holocaust and which forms the epigraph to "Yossel Rakover": "I believe in God even when He is silent."

Kolitz rightly rejects all those pseudo-prophets who presume to be privy to some secret divine knowledge when they describe the suffering of Jews in the Holocaust as punishment, and then proceed to define the "sins" which supposedly invited it. He angrily dismisses all the petty preachers of punishment who compound the sufferings of the victims of such unprecedented magnitude by blaming them for their own pain and humiliation:

"For saying that we deserve the blows we have received is to ourselves malign the Holy Name of God's children. And those who desecrate our name desecrate the name of the Lord; God is maligned by our self-deprecation."

The large themes which engage Kolitz are obviously universal, but that by no means obliterates or even overshadows the specifically Jewish element. Yossel Rakover speaks as a "simple living person who had the great but tragic honor of being a Jew":

I am proud that I am a Jew not in spite of the world's treatment of us, but precisely because of this treatment. I should be ashamed to belong to the people who spawned and raised the criminals who are responsible for the deeds that have been perpetrated against us.

Kolitz here adds an interesting thought: "I am proud to be a Jew because it is an art to be a Jew." Jewishness is an inborn trait. "One is born a Jew exactly as one is born an artist." By means of this aesthetic simile, Kolitz not only states explicitly that Jewishness is as inescapable for the Jew as art for the artist, but also, by implication, that both art and Jewishness require expression, working at it.

Emmanuel Levinas, in his essay, says a great deal that is both true and engaging in focusing on a critical passage that is inexplicably omitted in some English translations of "Yossel Rakover" (which also fail to mention Kolitz's name as the author!), "I love Him, but I love His Torah more, and even if I had deceived myself in this regard, I would nonetheless cling to His Torah." There are those who have maintained that this spurious interpretation transforms Kolitz's Yossel Rakover from a pious Hasid to a crypto-secularist. But this argument is more clever than correct, for the real sentiment is clearly there, and, moreover, it has deep roots in the classical Jewish tradition.

Thus, in Kolitz's original text, shortly after Yossel Rakover refers to the "art" of being Jewish, we read, "My relationship to You is not the relationship of a slave to his master, but rather that of a pupil to his teacher." Magisterial relationship of this kind self-evidently requires a teaching, whether oral or written, and poignantly expresses the relationship of the Jew to his God through the medium of Torah, a word which, quite literally, means "the Teaching." Yossel Rakover is a pious Jew, a Hasid; and even though Hasidism takes a different view of the relative value of the study of the sacred texts, on the one hand, and conscious and emotional religious experience, on the other, it has never denied the centrality of Torah and its significance as a, indeed the, medium for the encounter between God and man. Rabbi Israel Baal Shem Tov, the eighteenth-century founder of the Hasidic movement, taught that divinity inheres in the very words of the sacred text.

Kolitz is on solid ground in identifying the relation between the Jew and his God as that of student and teacher. It was none other than the prophet Isaiah who said, "and all thy children shall be taught of the Lord" (54:13). God is the Teacher, Israel is the pupil, and the Torah is the text. The metaphor is more than a literary device; it informs us that even during the cold, dark, brutal days and years of *hester panim*—when God's face is hidden and He seems unreachable, infinitely remote, and icily indifferent to our fate, frustrating our desire to experience His presence—the Text remains, and the bond between God and man holds.

The rabbinic tradition developed and cherished this theme. Thus, the sages of the Midrash paraphrased "And they have forsaken Me and not kept My Torah" (Jer. 16:11) to read, "Would that they forsake Me, [as long as] they keep My Torah [because its inner light will restore them to (the path of) righteousness]" (Lamentations Rabbah, introduction, 3). Palpable darkness may reign in the world, but the promise of redemption, the seeds of divine illumination and spiritual enlightenment, are present in the holy text.

In a time of *hester panim,* when God "has sacrificed humankind to its wild instincts," as Kolitz writes, it is not God who reveals the Torah, but the Torah that reveals God. That is authentic Jewish doctrine; more, it is the distillate of millennial Jewish historical experience.

Caveat lector! The reader must know that in reading "Yossel Rakover," he or she is not judging the story; it judges the reader. One who reads this testament without feeling shattered, or without at least experiencing a deep shudder—a shudder that not only shakes his body but shakes up his prejudices, his sense of normalcy, the very premises on which he conducts the affairs of his daily life—is in deep psychic trouble, in need of therapy for ossified sensitivity and redemption from a hardening of the heart and paralysis of the spirit.

But what this short piece evokes from the reader is more than profound sadness mingled with admiration for courage. It also engages the mind by revealing the range of thought and existential reactions of an authentically religious personality confronting ultimate questions that are not so much "theological" as "spiritual"—the best or only way to describe the profoundly religious ruminations of a man of faith facing the nadir of human depravity. Yossel Rakover/Zvi Kolitz speaks not as a philosopher but as a believer, not with theological sophistication but with an authentically human wisdom that is, at one and the same time, both assertive and humble. It is the reader—far from the events here described and safe from the flames licking at the ghetto charnel house—who must now translate these stirring ruminations and sentiments into a vocabulary more familiar to his quotidian affairs. Something will no doubt be gained by this act of translation; unfortunately, much more will be lost. But the experience of "getting into" Zvi Kolitz's "Yossel Rakover Speaks to God" is an adventure well worth the effort.

Prefatory Note

✿

Zvi Kolitz

On the occasion of the fiftieth anniversary of the Warsaw ghetto uprising, the *Frankfurter Allgemeine Zeitung,* one of Germany's oldest and most prestigious newspapers, published a German translation of "Yossel Rakover Speaks to God," prefaced by a feature article about the author and his story which was written by a member of its editorial staff, Paul Badde. Mr. Badde, who came all the way from Germany to interview me in New York, was not only, as he put it when he first contacted me by phone, "under the spell of the story," but, as I soon came to realize, under the reportorial obligation to find out how it had come to pass that long after I had first published the story as fiction, it was republished in various lands, including Israel, as an authentic testament discovered in the ruins of the Warsaw ghetto. Mr. Badde, with the thoroughness of an investigative reporter and the passion of a crusader, went to great lengths to trace the genealogy of a mistaken identity which had long caused me a great deal of frustration, and which, of course, I had protested and tried to correct whenever I was made aware of it, but not always successfully.

The reason must have been, as Abraham Sutzkever, the distinguished Yiddish poet, who had initially made the same mistake, put it to me—namely, that people simply refused to believe that the story could have been written by someone who had not been there. Once Mr. Badde had all the pieces of the puzzle in place, he wrote his comprehensive article, which was published in the magazine of the Sunday edition of the *Frankfurter Allgemeine Zeitung* on April 1, 1993.

In 1989, the Rev. Professor Frans van Beeck, who teaches theology at Loyola University in Chicago, published an impressive little volume titled *Loving the Torah More than God?* It contained the original Rakover story followed by an elaborate essay by Professor Emmanuel Levinas about the theologico-philosophical dimensions of the story as seen from the Judaic angle. Levinas's essay was followed by an evaluation of the story from the christological point of view. I should add that it was Professor Van Beeck, who is represented in this volume by a specially written piece, who first made me aware of the Levinas essay, which had been published in France and broadcast over French radio, as I later found out, ten years earlier! Professor Van Beeck also drew my attention to a passage in the Levinas essay which implies that though the story had been presented to him as a testament, as it had been to the two distinguished German writers whose meditations on the story are included in the volume, the French philosopher sensed, as it were, that it was a work of fiction.

★ ★ ★

The semi-documentary story "Requiem for a Jealous Boy" (first published in *Midstream* of April, 1989), with which I chose to conclude this volume, is somehow related to the question of "loving the Torah more than God." Dealing as it does with the supremacy of Torah over "religion" even in Auschwitz, let alone in Judaism, it may help to illustrate the actually lived truth of the fictitious Yossel Rakover's seemingly controversial statement. Only a religion preoccupied, not with dogma, but with din ("law") could have produced the kind of soulful, Torah-jealous boy to whom the requiem is dedicated.

Zvi Kolitz

✣

Paul Badde

"Yes?!" The wire crackles a little. "Mr. Kolitz?" "Yes." "Zvi Kolitz?" "Yes." "Are you the man who wrote 'Yossel Rakover'?" "Yes."

Did I fall silent? I hear a slight cough at the other end of the wire, across the Atlantic. "Who are you?" he asks. I tell him. Of course I can come and visit him, any time. I falter again.

That was four weeks ago. Everything I knew about the man had led me to assume that he was long dead. That is why I had asked an acquaintance in New York, where I knew he had lived in the fifties, to find his grave in Manhattan or perhaps in Brooklyn. "Impossible!" she had replied. "And anyway, Zvi Kolitz? Who is he supposed to have been?" But a day later she sends through his complete address on Central Park South from the telephone book, where she has found him, between a Kolitz, David on 65th Street and a Kolivas, Nicholas on 87th Street.

Seven days later we sit opposite each other in his apartment. A barrage of honking car-horns surges up weakly from the depths of Columbus Circle. Zvi Kolitz, very much alive, is almost lost in the brocade armchair from which he regards me searchingly, with a painting of a snow-covered town in Eastern Europe above him. From Lithuania he has ended up here—and Yossel Rakover came

1

out of burning Warsaw. I too had never heard these names until a friend discovered them for me six months ago: the creator and the creature respectively of a forgotten text-of-the-century, four pages long, a story that keeps getting lost again and again. There are few other tales about which so many tears have been shed. Why wasn't it in any of my school texts? It's a piece of fiction that breaks out of the framework of literature with the force of a hand grenade, as intensive as if it were from Shakespeare, and as serious and powerful as if Job himself had written it.

Yet it is Zvi Kolitz who wrote this story, Zvi Kolitz and no one else. I study him furtively while he tells me about his life. I had been told that he was peculiar, very strange: "a man with a bizarre path through life and a chaotic-genial temperament." His other writings were "insignificant"; only "Yossel Rakover" was a "unique work and great success, a sort of Marseillaise" (as if two such texts could be written in one lifetime).

What I knew and did not know I had mainly learned from Anna Maria Jokl, who now lives in Jerusalem. Paradoxically, she had translated him from Yiddish into German in 1954 before she ever discovered him. "Watch out!" she now warns me over the telephone in an old Bohemian tone of voice: "This story is full of traps!" "Where did you get it from, what you have written?" she asked Zvi Kolitz in a letter in 1955: "Who are you?" "I am a believing Jew," he answered at that time, "who would, however, say to God, should he ever meet Him, things that would make His hair stand on end."

Now, in an accent which has never really been polished away, he tells of his father, a rabbi and Talmud scholar at whose feet he grew up, and of his village home in Lithuania. He radiates with affection. "Six thousand Jews there were, and not one of them illiterate. To this day I can still hear them singing, chanting the Psalms on the Sabbath." His father died in 1930 at the age of forty-four, when Zvi was twelve. "My youth was happy," he says, passing over to memories of his mother, who came from Eydt-kuhnen on the Prussian-Lithuanian border and taught him and his siblings German poems. Yet at home they spoke Yiddish and in addition Hebrew; they were Zionists from childhood onwards.

The whole of Lithuania was cruelly antisemitic, he remembers. In 1937, at the age of nineteen, we see him and his family crossing through a delirious Germany on the way to Florence because, as a Jew, at home he is not allowed to go to study history at the university. In the harbor of Trieste he says farewell to his family, who leave for Palestine. They have recognized the signs of the times. Later he hears that all the inhabitants of his hometown have been burnt alive.

He himself only arrives in Palestine at the outbreak of World War II, via Venice and Alexandria. His time of apprenticeship is finished. He at once becomes involved in the Revisionist movement of Vladimir Jabotinsky, who seeks uncompromisingly to set up a Jewish state, and in the Irgun underground army, which wants to bomb the English out of the land. For this, the Florentine history student twice lands in prison. As if it were yesterday he remembers Rommel's advance on Palestine via North Africa, and Radio Crete's hourly announcements that the Swastika would soon be flying over the Tower of David in Jerusalem. In the King David Hotel in those days, there was an endless queue of kings and queens from all over the world. "The city had become a sanctuary for kings, while we were working out plans for withdrawing to the caves near the Dead Sea when the Wehrmacht attacked. The Polish general Anders also came into the country from Siberia and brought with him Menachem Begin, who became commander of the Irgun." In 1942 the members of the Jabotinsky movement joined the British Army on tactical grounds, in order to concentrate all forces against the Nazis.

At the beginning of the Passover feast in 1943, when the SS attacks the surrounded ghetto of far-off Warsaw with flame throwers, when for the first time since the days of Masada, Jews with weapons in their hands have risen up against their powerful oppressors, Zvi Kolitz is wearing the uniform of a British chief recruiting officer in Jerusalem. He has been released from a British jail in time to take up this post. For the duration of the war he travels in Egypt, Palestine, and the whole of the Middle East in order to recruit Jews as soldiers for the English. "For me, the British were gentlemen, even when I was sitting in their prisons." Now he himself sits in his armchair like a retired British colonel, with a last, thinning fringe of hair behind his temples, a fascinatingly courteous gentleman. Even his accent still carries some British traces.

In those days he was already working as a journalist, writing for the daily *Haboker* and weekly magazines, and publishing a book of Hebrew short stories: "A naive book about the events in Europe; in Israel we knew nothing until 1943." From then on, however, rumors fluttered like swarms of black ravens all over the land. Rumors that there are mass murders in Poland. Rumors that the leaders of the Jewish Agency are suppressing the truth in order not to undermine the war effort—heaps of very black rumors, increasing from year to year. "In 1943 we knew that something was going on, in 1944 we knew it for sure, yet by no means the full extent." He falls silent. "I remember," he then continues, "how at a meeting we talked about whether the rumors could be true. Some stood up and said that they didn't believe them. And then one man jumped up, Itzchak Grienbaum, a member of the Polish Parliament, hammering with his fists on the table and shrieking: 'They are annihilating us in masses in Poland!' I don't know why we didn't believe him. Because he was from the Left, because he was an atheist? I don't know. I never heard the word 'gas-chamber' before 1945."

After the war, Kolitz finds himself in a British jail again, and then we see him on his travels once more, almost always with two missions, one official and the other secret. He continues to be campaigner and recruiting expert, more active than ever, but now for a nascent state. In 1946, at the age of twenty-eight, he goes to Basel as a delegate to the World Zionist Congress, and shortly afterwards to Buenos Aires. This city too is full of rumors. Only a year before, Argentina had declared war on Germany and won immediately. Now, night after night, in addition to the important Jewish community, a growing crowd of escaped

Nazis streams into the German sections of Buenos Aires. At the Rio de la Plata, in the port, SS Obersturmbannführer Adolf Eichmann has disembarked unrecognized: the "final solver of the Jewish question." Peron becomes dictator.

"Argentina's Jews at that time were just beginning to realize what had happened in Europe. I talked every evening about what we could do: that the only help would be the creation of a Jewish state." He clears his throat. "There were 80,000 Jews living in Buenos Aires alone. And now, I remember it exactly, between two speeches which I had to give, a Señor Mordechai Stoliar, the editor of a local Yiddish daily, came to me and asked if I would write something for their Yom Kippur issue. It was called the *Yidishe Tsaytung.* Sounds almost German, doesn't it? I said: Yes, I have something in my mind which I've been wanting to write for a long time." In Warsaw, shortly beforehand, buried in bottles, the notes of Emanuel Ringelblum, whose chronicle of the ghetto had ended in December 1942 with the words "Our submission has led to nothing. Never should anything like this be allowed to happen again," had been discovered.

Thus it comes about that Zvi Kolitz, in his hotel room, begins writing "Yossel Rakover" that very evening. "I was alone. It was the City Hotel in Buenos Aires, and I remember that I did the end first. Then I had to think about it, between the many speeches I gave every evening. But I certainly remember that I wrote the end at the beginning and the beginning at the end. I needed a couple of days to lead the story back to the ending: a whole lifetime." He pauses. "This was before there was a State of Israel." It is the tremendous historical tension between the Warsaw uprising and the founding of the State of Israel which we see the young Irgun agent record in his notebooks. A prophetic sign. Does he realize this?

"Always, again and again, I remember my father telling us that the whole history of Israel is reflected in the history of Jacob at the river Jabbok. In advance, yes! Jacob was alone. And someone wrestled with him until daybreak, at last saying to him: 'Let me go! You shall no longer be called Jacob, but Israel, for you have wrestled with God and won.' This wrestling, I thought, came to a new climax in the Warsaw ghetto. Jacob knew he had no chance. Why did he wrestle with God nonetheless? It was absurd."

He stands up, folds his arms, and turns away. Whether he was paid in dollars for "Yossel Rakover" or in Argentine pesos, how much he got for his story, he has forgotten. Does he still have the newspaper from Buenos Aires? "Of course, I must still have it here somewhere. I will give it to you." And then what happened? "Well, the response was moving, and I thought: that's it. A year later I once again published the story in New York, translated into English, in an anthology that was soon out of print; and that was finally that."

That was not that at all. But it's true that since then his life has continued along two different lines: on the one hand as a personal biography, and on the other as the development of "Yossel Rakover" as "the story of a story," a short mystery melodrama. One thinks of a upside-down version of the Pirandello play in which six characters seek an author; this story tries, again and again, to shake off its author. Paradoxically, Zvi Kolitz's life is almost more quickly sketched than the life of the character he once created—although Kolitz, too, has led different lives: as a journalist, writer, campaigner, speaker, film-maker, businessman, producer. What hasn't he been? He was not a theologian; he has only become that with age.

His greatest success is a film, *Hill 24 Does Not Answer*. It was the first film from the young State of Israel to win international awards in Cannes and Mexico. He has also written six books. I leaf through them and am surprised that they are out of print. On Broadway he has produced spectacular plays like Rolf Hochhuth's *The Deputy* and musicals. Zvi Kolitz continues to write a weekly column for a Yiddish dally. Every Wednesday he gives a lecture at Yeshiva University. "Nothing is as seductive as success," he says about his early life in America. "At that time, the success of my film lured me away from Israel." I had heard that a close friend of Begin's had quarreled with him and that is why he left. "No," says Kolitz's second wife, Mathilda, facetiously, "I believe he moved away from Israel for my sake; I don't speak Hebrew."

Be that as it may, on this path he suddenly and unexpectedly again crosses the life's path of Yossel Rakover. While in America to introduce his film, he learns from the New York Yiddish press that in Israel they are still arguing over the question of whether Yossel Rakover's speech is an authentic document from the Warsaw ghetto or the product of an imagination, and whether the author is alive or dead. "It puzzled me completely. I couldn't understand it at all. I had written and declared this story a piece of fiction years ago, a *dertseylung,* as they say in Yiddish, and had only published it in Argentina and New York, never in Israel. I had never denied my name, either. Of course I was alive not dead. So I just didn't understand it. Beforehand I had spent some time with Ben-Gurion in the desert and only read the Hebrew but not the Yiddish press in Israel." He laughs briefly. "So I called the newspaper and wrote them a letter, saying: 'I don't understand.'"

But by then, years later, Yossel Rakover had taken on a life of his own after having shaken off his author the first time. In 1953 an unknown person in Argentina had sent a typewritten "Will from the Warsaw Ghetto" to *Di Goldene Keyt* ("The Golden Chain") in Tel Aviv; in the spring of 1954 the fortnightly Yiddish paper printed it as an "authentic document." "This piece had haunted us so much," Avraham Sutzkever, a Yiddish poet from the Vilna ghetto and the paper's editor, will later confess: "It seemed so genuine that we didn't even think to make any inquiries about it." Zvi Kolitz's correction not only came too late, it also came inconveniently, very inopportunely—and to no effect. In January 1955 the "discovered document" is broadcast in the German version of Anna Maria Jokl by Radio Free Berlin. Two months later it appears anonymously again, in a French translation, in *La terre retrouvée,* a Zionist magazine in Paris. The response is tremendous. Thomas Mann hears it on the radio shortly before his death and praises it as a holy text, a "shattering human and religious document." Rudolf Krämer-Badoni, then one of Germany's foremost writers, pens a moving response to Yossel Rakover, whose ashes he assumes to be mixed with the ashes of Warsaw: "I have just read your letter. How great your God must be, who awakes such souls in man!"

Even greater than this response is the furious protest and tumult triggered by the letters of the unknown Zvi Kolitz, not from the hereafter but from New York. Kolitz confesses to the authorship of Yossel Rakover's letter and to being an ordinary flesh-and-blood author, still living, who has never even visited Warsaw. This shall not be forgiven him! Anyone can come and claim credit, cry Kolitz's critics. Soon, someone will come and claim that Auschwitz too was invented. Imposter! Fraud! Rogue! These are just a few of the accusations hurled at Kolitz.

And if Kolitz was telling the truth, the text itself would now have to be regarded quite differently! It didn't help that Anna Maria Jokl pointed out at the time: "What do we know, after all, about what the man looked like who wrote the Book of Job?"

With the author's full and correct name, "Yossel Rakover Speaks to God" was broadcast once more in October 1955; later, Anna Maria Jokl reported on it at length in the *Tagesspiegel,* and the following year, for the first time, she published her radio manuscript with a commentary in the *Neue Deutsche Hefte.* Yet seven years later the Lithuanian philosopher Emmanuel Levinas published a wonderful essay in France about a text by an "anonymous author" which had been found, and which "was just as beautiful as it is real, as real as only real literature can be."

Two years on, in 1965, the story appears for the first time in a Hebrew translation, again merely as "testament," in *Ani Ma'min* in Jerusalem. Again Mr. Kolitz disclaims in a friendly fashion and at length. Three years later the story appears in a New York anthology under his name, but with the addendum that although it is not an authentic document, "there was indeed a Yossel Rakover who died in the flames in Warsaw," about whose fate the author had heard. None of this is true.

In the mid-seventies a book is published in Israel which reports that "'Yossel Rakover,' an anonymous document from the Warsaw Ghetto" has become the constitutional charter of Gush Emunim, a radical settlers' movement, where the text is read over and over again. In America it is inserted into the prayer books of Orthodox and Reform congregations for ceremonial readings. "Friends who know the story have reported to me," says Zvi Kolitz, "how in a large Conservative synagogue on 89th Street in Manhattan, the rabbi introduced a well-known actor who would now read a text which had been found in the Warsaw Ghetto. And he read 'Yossel Rakover.' The people wept. Afterwards my friends went to the rabbi and said: 'Rabbi, how can this be? We know the author.' He said, 'I too know that there is an author. But it's more moving this way.' That was perhaps five or six years ago. It's frightening. It bothers me, and makes me uneasy."

To increase the contradictions, nearly every published version has appeared in a different form; each deviates more or less sharply from the others, and practically all of them from the original. A few weeks ago Kolitz was asked for permission for a new translation from Danish into Swedish. Because he has never read any of the new versions properly, not even the translations for which he paid, new speculations—and doubts—have spread about his authorship. His attitude has never been that of a writer who knows his own text by heart. Critics find this incomprehensible.

A silver-framed photo on a bureau shows him in the fifties in Mexico in a white linen or silk suit, looking like Porfirio Rubirosa or Carlos Gardel, the legendary, elegant tango king. It is a photo of an outrageously good-looking young man, a playboy or adventurer. He may have been the one; he was certainly the other. Yet even at that time he ate only kosher foods, and now, according to his wife, he only drinks kosher wine. With Isaac Bashevis Singer, who for years lived a few blocks away from him, he always spoke Yiddish exclusively. He attended readings of Singer's work as often as he could. It was at one of them, some years ago, that he heard the Nobel Prize winner being asked about his attitude to the Holocaust. Singer said that anyone who wanted to know how he felt about the Holocaust should read "Yossel Rakover ret tsu Got!" "He thought just like this, like Yossel! I couldn't believe my ears. Just like Jacob at the river Jabbok."

Yet Jacob went away both blessed and wounded. "What is the blessing, you ask? And the wound? I'll tell you what the blessing and the wound are. The wound is the blessing! I am a very happy man!" Zvi Kolitz breathes deeply. He turns his head away. "I don't want to make a cult out of suffering. But nevertheless, happiness without suffering is a curse! Wait." He jumps up and goes to the bookcase: "I must read this aloud to you, from Kazantzakis's account of his journey to Mount Sinai." He puts on his glasses and turns the pages backwards and forwards: "Listen: 'Do you remember how he talks with the people? Have you seen how mountains and men are ground in the palm of his hand? Have you seen how kingdoms act at his feet? Man cries out, weeps, resists, hides under rocks, burrows underground. He struggles to elude him. But Jehovah is nailed to his loins like a knife.'" He opens his slim hand: "That is the wound. Our mission is tied up with it! It is the existential wound of which Heidegger speaks, and about which the Jews know so much more than any other people in the world: the wound of existence. I lost not one single person in Auschwitz, and yet not a single day goes by on which I don't think about Auschwitz. I have become incapable of not taking any sort of tragedy personally, wherever it happens. Take the daily newspaper. Every day is a wound."

Yes, he probably has had a happy life. Apart from his eldest brother Louis, who lost his life as an Air Force captain in the war against Hitler, there have been no violent deaths in his family. Just a few weeks ago, Zvi Kolitz, who is a father and a grandfather, lost his brother Chaim, only eight years ago his mother, and then two sisters. Two other sisters live in Israel. The elder, a former beauty queen of Lithuania, is a therapist for respiratory ailments in Tel Aviv. Rachel, the younger, I consider alongside the sister of Yeshayahu Leibowitz to be the country's greatest scriptural scholar. Itzchak, his youngest brother, has been the chief rabbi of Jerusalem for the last ten years.

The glassy chime of a grandfather clock has divided our talk into a half-hourly rhythm and finally ends it. Kolitz's "Yossel Rakover" is a world success, but without him; it hasn't made him famous. "No," he says with self-assurance, "my life has not been altered or changed by Yossel Rakover. He was my creation; he was formed by a conviction in which I grew up. How can the creature change the spirit that created him?"

The original Argentine manuscript, or the Yom Kippur issue of the *Yidishe Tsaytung,* which he wanted to give me, Kolitz can't find anywhere. I must forgive him; he is unfortunately terribly disorganized. A pity. I let my gaze wander once more through the neat, orderly apartment—over the bookcases, the little marble table, the carpets, the paintings, the fireplace—while as a substitute he dedicates another book to me with two friendly sentences. It is the very careful work of an eminent scholar from Chicago about "Yossel Rakover" and Emmanuel Levinas, who many years ago analyzed and interpreted the story like a psalm.

Yet is it possible that Mr. Kolitz has never read this book either? On the journey home, I leaf through it a bit and suddenly sit up straight as I begin to read how four years ago, in a brilliantly critical textual analysis, it was proved that the original was never written in Yiddish but in English and in New York. The book is, as the foreword correctly remarks, "an intellectual feast." Afterwards an "anonymous translator" rendered the text into Yiddish and offered it for publication in Tel Aviv to *Di Goldene Keyt.* But not only that. The translator significantly enlarged the text. Word for word the additions are proved and named. I look at them in detail and see and realize: They are all the climaxes of Yossel's argument with God.

After my return home, Professor Frans Jozef van Beeck of Loyola University, who wrote the book, gives me every imaginable assistance; I've never experienced such cooperation. His idea is fascinating. Doesn't it make the whole thing even better and more mysterious? Isn't the text—almost biblically!—a magnetic work which attracted adapters and editors on its way who then often contributed the best ideas? There is no Yiddish original from the year 1946! But if so, why didn't Zvi Kolitz tell me?

In Buenos Aires telephone information no longer knows the *Yidishe Tsaytung* (but there are thousands of Señor Stoliars; which of them should I ask?). And from Berlin to New York, no Jewish library can help with a copy or even a microfilm of the mysterious paper. I call the Jesuit College in the Argentine capital on the off-chance they'll have some information. An unknown Father Oscar Lateur picks up the receiver. He can't help either, how could he? My article must be finished; I have already failed to make the deadline. Discouraged, I open the newspaper and look at today's wounds: the mutilation of Bosnia, the shadows of the Four Horsemen of the Apocalypse over Russia, the deadly spiral of pre-Easter terror in Palestine, plans to electrify the barbed wire around the Gaza Strip. Suddenly the fax comes to life, there is a soft purring. I read B-u-e-n-o-s A-i-r-e-s as the first page leaves the machine. It is a chaotic, stuck-together article in Hebrew letters. Only the headline appears in Latin letters: "EL DIARIO ISRAELITA — Miércoles 25 de Setiembre 1946." Gigantic blots of ink decorate each page. The pages are blotchy, here too dark, here too pale, here and there a bit missing, and yet it is clearly legible: "YOSSEL RAKOVERS VENDUNG TSU G-OT — Dertseylung fun ZVI KOLITZ far di Yidishe Tsaytung." There follows an indecipherable introduction, then in clearer fragments: "In eyner fun warschawer geto, tsvishn hoyfns fun farsmolyete shteyner und mentshlekhe beyner is qefunen gevorn . . . di vayterdike tsavoe geshribn fun a jidn . . ." And further on, quite clearly: "Varshe, dem 28stn april 1943 — Ikh, Yossel, der zun fun David Rakover fun Tarnopol, a khosid fun gerer rebn un opshtamiker fun di tsadikim gadoylim un kadoyshim fun di mishpokhes Rakover un Mayzls, shrayb di dosike shures, ven dos Varshaver geto is in flamen . . . "

Yossel Rakover Speaks to God

✡

Zvi Kolitz

I believe in the sun even when it is not shining, I believe in love even when feeling it not; I believe in God even when He is silent.

—inscription on the wall of a cellar
in Cologne where a number of Jews
hid for the entire duration of the war

In the ruins of the ghetto of Warsaw, among heaps of charred rubbish, there was found, packed tightly into a small bottle, the following testament, written during the ghetto's last hours by a Jew named Yossel Rakover.

Warsaw, April 28, 1943
I, Yossel, son of Dovid Rakover of Tarnopol, a Hasid of the Rebbe of Ger and a descendant of the righteous, learned, and God-fearing families of Rakover and Meisels, am writing these lines as the houses of the Warsaw ghetto go up in flames. The house I am in is one of the few still not burned. For several hours an unusually heavy artillery barrage has been crashing down on us, and the walls around me are crumbling and disintegrating under the con-

13

centrated fire. Before long the house I am in will be transformed, like almost every other house in the ghetto, into a grave
for its defenders. By the dagger-sharp, unusually crimson rays of
the sun that penetrate through the small, half-walled-up window
of my room, through which we have been shooting at the enemy
day and night, I see that it must now be late afternoon, just
before sundown, and the sun probably has no idea how little I
regret that I will not see it again. Something peculiar has happened to us; all our notions and emotions have changed. Death,
swift and abrupt, looks like a savior to us, like a liberator, break-
ing our shackles; and beasts of the field seem so lovable and dear
that I feel deep pain whenever the evil fiends that dominate
Europe are referred to as beasts. It is not true that there is something beastly in Hitler. He is, I am deeply convinced, a typical
child of modern man. Humanity as a whole has spawned him
and reared him, and he is the frankest expression of its innermost, most deeply buried wishes.

In a forest where I once hid, I encountered a dog one night,
sick and starving; perhaps mad as well, his tail between his legs.
Both of us immediately felt the kinship, if not in fact the similarity, of our situations, because the situation of a stray dog is not,
by and large, much better than ours. He cuddled up to me, buried his head in my lap, and licked my hands. I do not know
whether I ever cried so much as that night. I threw my arms
around his neck, crying like a baby. If I say that I envied the ani-
mals at that moment, it would be no wonder. But what I felt was
more than envy. It was shame. I felt ashamed in front of the dog
to be, not a dog, but a man. That is how it is. That is the spiritual
state to which we have come. Life is a tragedy, death a savior;
man a calamity, the beast an ideal; day a horror, night—a relief.

Millions of people in the great wide world, who love the day,
the sun, and the light, do not know, do not have the slightest
idea, how much darkness and unhappiness the sun has brought
us. It has been turned into a tool in the hands of the evildoers,
and they have used it as a searchlight, to track the footprints of
those who are fleeing.

When my wife, my six children, and I hid in the forest, it was night, and night alone, that concealed us in its bosom. Day turned us over to those who were seeking our lives. How can I ever forget the day when the Germans raked with a hail of fire the thousands of refugees on the highway from Grodno to Warsaw? As the sun rose, the airplanes zoomed over us. The whole day long, without letup, they murdered us. In this massacre from the sky, my wife perished, with our seven-month-old child in her arms. Two more of my five remaining children disappeared that day without a trace. Their names were Dovid and Yehuda, one was four years old, the other six.

At sunset, the handful of survivors continued their journey toward Warsaw, and I, with my three remaining children, started out to comb the fields and woods at the site of the massacre in search of the children. "Dovid! Yehuda!"—so, throughout the night, our voices cut, as if with knives, the dead silence around us; and a forest echo, helpless, pitiful, and heart-rending, answered our cries, in tones of lamenting eulogy. I never saw my two children again, and in a dream I was told not to worry about them, because they were in the hands of *Ribono-shel-Oylom*.[1]

My other three children died in the course of a year in the Warsaw ghetto. Rokhele, my little daughter, ten years old, had heard that it was possible to find scraps of bread in the public dump outside the ghetto walls. The ghetto was starving at the time, and the bodies of those who died of starvation lay in the streets like heaps of rags. The people of the ghetto were prepared to face any death except death by starvation. This was because the desire to eat remains even after systematic persecution has destroyed all one's spiritual desires, and even if one wishes to die. I have heard about a half-starved Jew who once said to another: "If I could only have one meal like a human being, I would be willing to die!"

Rokhele told me nothing of her plan to steal out of the ghetto, a crime punishable by death. She and a girlfriend of the same

---

1. Lit. "Master of the World," i.e., God Almighty.

age started out on the perilous journey. They left home under cover of darkness, and at sunrise she and her friend were caught outside the ghetto walls. Nazi ghetto guards, together with dozens of their Polish underlings, at once started in pursuit of these two Jewish children who had dared to hunt for a piece of bread in a garbage can in order not to die of hunger. People witnessing the chase could not believe their eyes. Even in the ghetto it was unprecedented. One might have thought they were pursuing dangerous criminals. Dozens of fiends running amok after a pair of starved ten-year-old children who did not last very long. One of them, my child, running with her last ounce of strength, fell exhausted to the ground, and then the Nazis drove a bayonet through her head. The other girl saved herself, but, driven out of her mind, died two weeks later.

The fifth child, Yacob, a boy of thirteen, died of tuberculosis on his Bar Mitzvah day, and his death was a deliverance for him. The last child, my fifteen-year-old daughter Khave, perished during a *Kinderaktion*[2] that began at sunrise last Rosh Hashona and ended at sunset. That day, before the sun went down, hundreds of Jewish families had lost their children.

Now my time has come. And like Job, I can say of myself—nor am I the only one who can say this—that I return to the soil naked, as naked as on the day of my birth.

I am forty-three years old, and when I look back on the past I can assert confidently, as confidently as a man can be in judging himself, that I have lived an honest life, and that my heart was full of love. At one time I was blessed with success, but I never boasted about it. I had many possessions and, as my rebbe used to say, very rarely had to make sacrifices. By law and by faith, if I had ever been tempted to steal, it would only have been so as to enjoy depravity for its own sake. My house was open to the needy, and I was happy whenever I was able to do anyone a favor. I served God enthusiastically, and my sole request to Him

---

2. Lit. "children's action"; a roundup of Jewish children.

was that He allow me to worship Him *bikhol livovekho, bikhol nafshekho ubikhol miodekho.*[3]

After everything I have lived through, I cannot say that my relationship to God remains unchanged, but I can say with absolute certainty that my belief in Him has not changed a hair's breadth. In the past, when I was well and well off, my relation to God was as to one who kept on granting me favors for which I was always indebted; now my relationship to Him is as to one who owes me something, owes me much. And since I feel that He owes me something, I believe that I have the right to demand it of Him. But I do not say, like Job, that God should point a finger at my sin so that I may know why I deserve this; for bigger and better people than I are firmly convinced that what is now happening is not a question of punishment for transgressions but rather that something very specific is taking place in the world. More exactly, it is a time of *hester ponim.*[4]

God has veiled His countenance from the world, and thus has delivered mankind over to its most savage impulses. And unfortunately, when the power of impulse dominates the world, it is quite natural that the first victims should be those who embody the divine and the pure. Speaking personally, this is hardly a consolation, but since the destiny of our people is determined, not by earthly, material, and physical calculations, but by calculations not of this earth, spiritual and divine, the believer should see such events as a fragment of a great divine reckoning, against which human tragedies do not count for much. This, however, does not mean that the pious of my people should justify the edict by claiming that God and God's judgments are right. I believe that to say we deserve the blows we have received is to malign ourselves, to desecrate the *Shem hamfoyrosh*[5] "Jew," and

---

3. "With all your heart, and with all your soul, and with all your might" (Deut. 6:5), a biblical quotation included in the Shema prayer, the profession of faith recited twice daily by observant Jews.

4. God's "Veiling of His Countenance."

5. Lit. "The Ineffable Name," a phrase usually referring to God, but here applied to the ordinary Jew.

this is the same as desecrating the actual *Shem hamfoyrosh*—God; God is maligned when we malign ourselves.

In a situation like this, I naturally expect no miracles, nor do I ask Him, my Lord, to show me mercy. May He treat me with the same countenance-veiling indifference with which He has treated millions of His people. I am no exception, and I expect no special treatment. I will no longer attempt to save myself, nor flee any more. I will facilitate the work of the fire by moistening my clothing with gasoline. I have three bottles of gasoline left after having poured several dozen on the heads of the murderers. That was one of the finest moments in my life, and I roared with laughter. I had never dreamed that the death of human beings, even of enemies—even of such enemies—could so delight me. Foolish humanists may say what they like. Vengeance was and always will be the last means of waging battle and the greatest emotional gratification of the oppressed. Until now I never understood the precise meaning of the passage in the Talmud that states: "Vengeance is sacred because it is mentioned between two of God's names; as it is written: 'A God of vengeance is the Lord.'"[6] Now I understand it. Now I know why my heart is so overjoyed when I recall that for thousands of years we have been calling our Lord a God of vengeance: "A God of vengeance is our Lord."

Now that I am in a position to see life with particularly clear eyes—something only rarely given people before death—it seems to me that there is a fundamental difference between our God and the God in whom the nations of Europe believe. Our God is a God of vengeance, and our Torah is full of death penalties for the seemingly smallest sins, yet at the same time the Talmud relates that it was enough for the Sanhedrin, the highest tribunal of our people when it was free in its own land, to sentence a person to death once in seventy years to have the judges considered murderers.[7] In contrast, the followers of the God of

6. Berakhot 33a, citing Ps. 94:1.
7. See Mishnah Makkot 1:20, Talmud Bavli Makkot 7a.

the nations, the so-called God of love, who commanded them to love every creature made in the divine image, have been murdering us without pity, day in, day out, for almost two thousand years.

Yes, I have spoken of vengeance. We have had only a few opportunities to see true vengeance. But when we saw it, it was so good and so worthwhile to see, I felt such deep satisfaction, such tremendous pleasure, that it seemed as if an entirely new life was springing up in me. A tank had suddenly broken into our street. It was bombarded with flaming bottles of gasoline from all the embattled houses. They failed to hit their target, however, and the tank continued on its way. I and my friends waited until the tank was literally passing under our noses. Then, through the half-bricked-up window, we suddenly attacked. The tank burst into flames, and six blazing Nazis jumped out. Ah, how they burned! They burned like the Jews they had set on fire, but they screamed more. Jews do not scream. They accept death as a savior. The Warsaw ghetto perishes in battle. It perishes shooting, struggling, blazing, but no, not screaming!

I still have three bottles of gasoline, and they are as precious to me as wine to a drunkard. After emptying one over my clothes, I will place the paper on which I write these lines in the bottle and hide it among the bricks of the half-walled-up window of this room. If anyone ever finds it and reads it, he will, perhaps, understand the emotions of one of the millions of Jews who died forsaken by the God in whom he believed unshakably. I will let the two other bottles explode on the heads of the evildoers when my last moment comes.

There were twelve of us in this room at the outbreak of the revolt. For nine days we battled against the enemy. All eleven of my comrades have fallen, dying silently. Even the little boy— God only knows how he got here—about five years old, who is now lying dead near me, with his lovely little face wearing the kind of smile that appears on the faces of children who are peacefully dreaming. Even this child died with the same epic calm as his older comrades. It happened early this morning. Most of us were already dead. The boy scaled the heap of corpses to catch a glimpse of the outside world through the window. For several minutes he stood beside me like that. Suddenly he fell backwards, rolling down the pile of corpses, and lay like a stone. On his small, pale forehead, between the locks of black hair, there was a spattering of blood.

Until sunrise yesterday, when the enemy opened a concentrated barrage against our bunker, one of the last in the ghetto, every one of us was still alive, although five were wounded, each of them still fighting nonetheless. Yesterday and today, all of them fell, one after the other, one on top of the other, standing at their posts and firing until shot to death.

Apart from the three bottles of gasoline, I have no more ammunition. There is still heavy firing from the three floors above me, but they cannot send any help, for the stairway has been destroyed by shellfire, and I think the house is about to cave in. I am lying on the floor as I write these lines, surrounded by my dead comrades. I look into their faces, and a quiet but mocking irony seems to animate them, as if they were saying, "Be patient, you foolish man, another few minutes and everything will become clear to you too." This irony particularly cries out from the face of the little boy lying at my right hand as if asleep. His tiny mouth is drawn into a smile exactly as if he were laughing, and I, who still live and feel and think like a being of flesh and blood—it seems to me that he is laughing at me. He is laughing with that quiet but eloquent, penetrating laughter characteristic of those who know a lot when they try to convey *true knowledge* to those who know *nothing* and think they know everything. Now he knows everything, the boy. It's all clear to him now. He even knows why he was born even though he had to die so soon, and why he died only five years after his birth. And even if he doesn't know why, at least he knows that whether or not he knows it is completely unimportant and insignificant in the light of the revelation of the divine glory in that better world where he now finds himself, perhaps in the arms of his murdered parents to whom he has returned. In an hour or two I too will make the same discovery. Unless my face is eaten away by the flames, a similar smile may rest on it after I am dead. Meanwhile, I am still alive, and before my death I would like to speak to my God as a living man, a simple, living man who has had the great but unfortunate honor of being a Jew.

I am proud that I am a Jew not *in spite of* the world's treatment of us, but precisely *because of* this treatment. I would be ashamed to belong to one of the peoples that spawned and raised the criminals who are responsible for the deeds that have been perpetrated against us.

I am proud to be a Jew because it is an *art* to be a Jew, because it is *hard* to be a Jew. It is no art to be an Englishman, an American, or a Frenchman. It may be easier, more comfortable, to be one of them, but not more honorable. Yes, it is an honor to be a Jew!

I believe that to be a Jew means to be a fighter, an everlasting swimmer against the turbulent, criminal human current. The Jew is a hero, a martyr; he is holy! You, our enemies, declare that we are bad. I believe that we are better and finer than you, but even if we were worse, I would like to see how you would look in our place!

I am happy to belong to the world's most unfortunate people, whose Torah represents the loftiest and most beautiful body of law and morality. This Torah has been made even holier and more immortal by the degradation and insult to which it has been subjected by the enemies of God.

I believe that to be a Jew is an inborn trait. One is born a Jew exactly as one is born an artist. It is impossible to be released from being a Jew. A divine attribute within us has made us a chosen people. Those who do not understand this will never understand the higher meaning of our martyrdom. "There is nothing more whole than a broken heart," a great rebbe once said,[8] and there is no people more chosen than a people permanently persecuted. If I did not believe that God once picked us

---

8. Rabbi Nahman of Bratslav (1772–1811); see Arthur Green, *Tormented Master: A Life of Rabbi Nahman of Bratslav* (New York: Schocken, 1981), p. 148.

to be a chosen people, I would believe that our tribulations have made us chosen.

I believe in Israel's God even if He has done everything to stop me from believing in Him. I believe in His laws even if I cannot justify His actions. My relationship to Him is no longer the relationship of a slave to his master but rather that of a student to his teacher. I bow my head before His greatness, but will not kiss the rod with which He strikes me.

I love Him, but I love His Torah more, and even if I were disappointed in Him, I would still observe His Torah. God means religion, but His Torah means a way of life, and the more we die for this way of life, the more sacred and immortal it becomes.

Therefore, my God, allow me, before death, being absolutely free of every semblance of terror, finding myself in a state of absolute inner peace and assurance, to argue things out with You for the last time in my life.

You say that we have sinned? Of course we have. And therefore that we are being punished? I can understand that too. But I would like You to tell me *whether any sin in the world deserves the kind of punishment we have received.*

You say that You will yet repay our enemies? I am convinced that You will. Repay them without mercy? I have no doubt of that either.

Nevertheless, I would like You to tell me *whether any punishment in the world can compensate for the crimes that have been committed against us?*

You say, perhaps, that it is no longer a question of sin and punishment, but a situation of *hester ponim* in which You have abandoned humanity to its impulses? Then I would like to ask You, God—and this question burns in me like a consuming fire—*What more, oh, what more must transpire for You to again reveal Your countenance?*

I want to tell You openly and clearly that now, more than in any previous period of our endless path of agony, do we have— we the tortured, the humiliated, the strangled, the buried alive and burned alive, we the insulted, the mocked, the ridiculed, the murdered by the millions—that now do we have the right to know *the limits of Your patience.*

I should like to tell You something else: Do not put the rope under too much strain, because, God forbid, it might snap. The test to which You have put us is so severe, so unbearably severe, that You should—You must—forgive those of Your people who, in their misery and rage, have turned away from You.

Forgive those who have turned from You in their misery, but also those who have turned from You in their happiness. You have transformed our lives into such an unending ordeal that the cowards among us have tried to avoid it, to run away from it any way they could. Do not strike them for it. One does not strike cowards, one pities them. And on them more than on us, O God, have mercy!

Forgive those who have desecrated Your name, who have gone over to the service of other gods, who have become indifferent to You. So severely have You struck them that they no longer believe You are their Father, that they have any Father at all.

I tell You this because I believe in You, because I believe in You more than ever, because now I know that You are my Lord, because surely You are not, surely You cannot be, the God of those whose deeds are the most horrible manifestation of god-lessness.

If You are not my God, whose God are You? The God of the murderers?

If those who hate me and murder me are so sinister, so evil, what then am I if not the one who reflects something of Your light, of Your goodness?

I cannot praise You for the deeds You tolerate. I bless and praise You, however, for the very fact of Your existence, for Your terrible greatness, which is so awesome that even what is happening now makes no impression on You! And precisely because You are so great and I so small, I pray You, I warn You in Your own name: stop underscoring Your greatness by tolerating the torments of the persecuted.

Nor am I asking You to strike down the guilty. It is the dreadful logic of the inexorable course of events that they will eventually strike themselves, for in our being killed the conscience of the world has been killed; in the murder of Israel a world has died.

The world will be devoured by its own evil, it will drown in its own blood.

The murderers have already passed sentence on themselves and will never escape it; but may You execute a sentence, a doubly severe sentence, on those who condone the crime.

Those who condemn the murder with their mouths, but rejoice at it in their hearts.

Those who meditate in their foul hearts: "Yes, he is evil, this tyrant, but he is doing a piece of work for us for which we will always be grateful!"

It is written in your Torah that a thief is to be punished more severely than a brigand, even though a thief does not attack his victim physically and merely attempts to take his possessions by stealth.

The reason is that the brigand, who attacks his victim in broad daylight, fears neither man nor God. But the thief fears man, not God.[9] That is why his punishment is more severe than the brigand's.

It would not bother me if You treated the murderers as You treat brigands, for their attitude toward You and toward us is the same, and they make no secret of their murders and their crimes.

But those who are silent in the face of murder, those who have no fear of You, but fear what people might say (fools! they are unaware that people will say nothing!), those who express sympathy for the drowning man but refuse to rescue him—punish them, O Lord, punish them; I implore You, punish them; I pray, punish them like thieves!

---

9. His criminal acts show that he does not fear God, but since he breaks in at night or when no one is home, it is obvious that he fears other human beings. See Baba Kamma 79b.

Death can wait no longer, and I must finish my writing. On the floors above me, the firing is growing weaker by the minute. The last defenders of this stronghold are now falling, and with them falls and perishes the great, beautiful, God-fearing Jewish Warsaw. The sun is about to set, and I thank God that I will never see it again. The red glow of the conflagrations comes in through the little window, and the bit of sky I can see is red and turbulent like a waterfall of blood. In about an hour at the most I will be with my family and with the millions of other dead members of my people in that better world where there are no more doubts, and where God alone is sovereign.

I die peacefully, but not complacently; persecuted, but not enslaved; embittered, but not cynical; a believer, but not a supplicant; a lover of God, but no blind amen-sayer.

I have followed Him even when He repulsed me. I have obeyed His commandments even when He has struck me for it; I have loved Him and will continue to love Him even when He has hurled me to the ground, tortured me to death, made me an object of shame and ridicule.

My rabbi always told the story of a Jew who fled from the Spanish Inquisition with his wife and child, striking out in a small boat on the stormy sea until he reached a rocky island. A bolt of lightning killed his wife; a storm rose and hurled his son into the sea. Alone, solitary as a stone, naked and barefoot, lashed by the storm and terrified by the thunder and lightning, with disheveled hair and hands outstretched to God, the Jew continued on his way across the desolate, rocky isle, turning to God with the following words:

"God of Israel, I have fled here in order to be able to serve You undisturbed, to follow Your commandments and sanctify Your name. You, however, do everything to make me stop believing in You. Now, lest it occur to You that by imposing these tribulations You will succeed in driving me from the right path, I notify You, my God and the God of my father, that it will not avail you in the least. You may insult me, You may strike me, You may take away all that I cherish and hold dear in the world, You may torture me to death—I will always believe in You, I will always love You! Yea, even in spite of You!

And these are my last words to You, my wrathful God: Nothing will avail You in the least! You have done everything to make me renounce You, to make me lose faith in You, but I die exactly as I have lived, an unshakable believer!

Praised forever be the God of the dead, the God of vengeance, truth, and law, who will soon show His face to the world again and shake its foundations with His almighty voice.

Hear, O Israel, the Lord our God, the Lord is One.[10]

Into your hands, O Lord, I commit my spirit.[11]

---

10. Deut. 6:4. The first line of the daily Shema, recited also as the conclusion of the Vidui, the deathbed confessional prayer.

11. Ps. 31:6. Recited as part of the Vidui.

To Love the Torah More Than God

⚜

Emmanuel Levinas

Among the recent publications devoted to Judaism in the West, there are a great many beautiful texts. Talent is not a problem in Europe. Rarely, however, are the texts real. Over the past one hundred years, Hebrew learning has faded, and we have lost touch with our sources. What learning is still being produced is based on an intellectual tradition; it remains self-taught and untutored, even when it is not improvised. And what worse corruption can befall an author than being read only by people who know less than he does! With no one to check them, no one to put them in their places, authors tend to mistake the lack of counterpressure for freedom, and this freedom for the touch of genius. Small wonder that the reading public remains skeptical; for them, Judaism, with its few million unrepentant adherents left in the world, is no more than a matter of quibbling over religious observances—something uninteresting and unimportant.

I have just read a text which is both beautiful and real—as real as only fiction can be. An anonymous author published it in an Israeli journal; under the title "Yossel, Son of Yossel [sic] Rakover of Tarnopol, Speaks to God," it was translated for *La terre retrouvée*, the Zionist paper in Paris, by Mr. Arnold Mandel, who, it would appear, read it with deep emotion. The text deserves even

27

more. It conveys an intellectual attitude that reflects something better than the reading habits of intellectuals—something superior to the handful of concepts borrowed, for instance, from Simone Weil, who, as everyone in Paris knows, is the latest fad in religious terminology. What this text provides is Jewish learning modestly understated, yet full of assurance; it represents a deep, authentic experience of the spiritual life.

The text presents itself as a document written during the last few hours of the resistance of the Warsaw Ghetto. The narrator is a witness to all the horrors. He has lost his young children under brutal circumstances. As his family's last survivor, and that for only a few more moments, he bequeaths to us his final thoughts. A literary fiction, certainly, but a fiction that affords each of us, as survivors, a dizzying view of ourselves and our lives.

I am not going to recount the whole tale, even though the world has learned nothing and forgotten everything. I pass when I am asked to stage the Passion of Passions as if it were a show; I refuse to derive any author's or theatrical director's glory from those inhuman cries. They resound and reverberate, never to be silenced, through the everlasting ages. Let us listen only to the thought that articulates itself in them.

What is the meaning of the suffering of the innocent? Does it not witness to a world without God, to an earth where only man determines the measure of good and evil? The simplest, most ordinary response would indeed be to draw the conclusion that there is no God. This would also be the healthiest response for all those who until now have believed in a rather primitive God who awards prizes, imposes sanctions, or pardons mistakes, and who, in His goodness, treats people like perpetual children. But what kind of limited spirit, what kind of strange magician did you project as the inhabitant of your heaven—you who today state that heaven is deserted? And why are you still looking, beneath an empty heaven, for a world that makes sense and is good?

Yossel son of Yossel experiences, with renewed vigor, beneath an empty heaven, certainty about God. For his finding himself thus alone allows him to feel, on his shoulders, all of God's responsibilities. On the road that leads to the one and only God, there is a way station without God. True monotheism must frame answers to the legitimate demands of atheism. An adult's God reveals Himself precisely in the emptiness of the child's heaven. That is (according to Yossel ben Yossel) the moment when God withdraws Himself from the world and veils His countenance. "He has sacrificed humankind to its wild instincts," says our text. "And because those instincts dominate the world, it is natural that those who preserve the divine and the pure should be the first victims of this domination."

God veiling His countenance: I think this is neither a theologian's abstraction nor a poetic image. It is the hour when the just person has nowhere to go in the outside world; when no institution affords him protection; when even the comforting sense of the divine presence, experienced in a childlike person's piety, is withdrawn; when the only victory available to the individual lies in his conscience, which necessarily means, in suffering. This is the specifically Jewish meaning of suffering—one that never takes on the quality of a mystical expiation for the sins of the world. The condition in which victims find themselves in a disordered world, that is to say, in a world where goodness does not succeed in being victorious, is suffering. This reveals a God who, while refusing to manifest Himself in any way as a help, directs His appeal to the full maturity of the integrally responsible person.

But by the same token this God who veils His countenance and abandons the just person, unvictorious, to his own justice—this faraway God—comes from inside. That is the intimacy that coincides, in one's conscience, with the pride of being Jewish, of being concretely, historically, altogether mindlessly, a part of the Jewish people. "To be a Jew means . . . to be an everlasting swimmer against the turbulent, criminal human current. . . . I am happy to belong to the unhappiest people in the world, to the people whose Torah represents the loftiest and most beautiful of all laws and moralities."

Intimacy with this virile God is attained in passing an ultimate test. Because I belong to the suffering Jewish people, the faraway God becomes my God. "Now I know that you are truly my God, for you cannot possibly be the God of those whose deeds are the most horrible expression of a militant absence of God." The just person's suffering for the sake of a justice that fails to triumph is concretely lived out in the form of Judaism. Israel—historical, carnal Israel—once again becomes a religious category.

God veiling His countenance and recognized as present and intimate: is He possible? Or are we dealing with a metaphysical construct, with a paradoxical *salto mortale* in the style of Kierkegaard? I think something very different manifests itself here, namely, the characteristic features of Judaism; the relationship between God and the human person is not an emotional communion within the context of the love of an incarnate God, but a relationship between minds that is mediated by teaching, by the Torah. The guarantee that there is a living God in our midst is precisely a word of God that is not incarnate. Trust in a God who does not reveal Himself through any worldly authority can rest only on inner clarity and on the quality of a teaching. There is nothing blind about it, much to the credit of Judaism. Hence this phrase of Yossel ben Yossel's, which is the highpoint of the entire monologue, echoing the whole Talmud: "I love Him, but I love His Torah even more. . . . And even if I had been deceived by Him and, as it were, disenchanted, I would nonetheless observe the precepts of the Torah." Blasphemy? Well, in any case a protection against the folly of a direct contact with the Sacred not based on reasonable grounds. But above all, a trust not based on the triumph of any institution, but on the inner clarity of the morality conveyed by the Torah. A difficult journey this, already being undertaken in spirit and truth, and which has nothing to prefigure! Simone Weil, you have never understood anything about the Torah! "Our God is a God of vengeance," says Yossel ben Yossel, "and our Torah is filled with death penalties for venial sins. And yet it was enough for the Sanhedrin, the highest tribunal of our people in its land, to sentence a person to death once in seventy years to have the judges considered murderers. On the other hand, the God of the Gentiles has commanded to love every creature made in his image, and in his name our blood has been poured out for almost two thousand years."

The true humanity of man and his virile tenderness come into the world along with the severe words of a demanding God; the spiritual becomes present, not by way of palpable presence, but by absence; God is concrete, not by means of incarnation, but by means of the Law, and His majesty is not the felt experience of His sacred mystery. His majesty does not provoke fear and trembling, but fills us with higher thoughts. To veil His countenance in order to demand—in a superhuman way—everything of man, to have created man capable of responding, of turning to his God as a creditor and not always as a debtor: that is truly divine majesty! After all, a creditor is one who has faith par excellence, but he is not going to resign himself to the subterfuges of the debtor. Our monologue opens and closes with this refusal to settle for resignation. Capable of trusting in an absent God, man is also the adult who can take the measure of his own weakness; if the heroic situation in which he stands validates the world, it also puts it in jeopardy. Matured by a faith derived from the Torah, he blames God for His unbounded majesty and His excessive demands. He will love God in spite of His every attempt to discourage his love. But, Yossel ben Yossel cries out, "do not put the bow under too much strain." Religious life cannot come to fruition in this heroic situation. God must unveil His countenance, justice and power must find each other again, just institutions are needed on this earth. But only the person who recognizes the veiled God can demand His revelation. How vigorous the dialectic by which the equality between God and man is established right at the heart of their incommensurability!

And thus we are as far removed from the warm, almost palpable communion with the divine as from the desperate pride of the atheist. An integral and austere humanism, coupled with difficult worship! And from the other point of view, a worship that coincides with the exaltation of man! A personal God, one God alone: that is not revealed as quickly as a slide shown in a dark room! The text I have commented on shows how ethics and the order of first principles combine to establish a personal relationship worthy of the name. To love the Torah more than God—this means precisely to find a personal God against whom it is possible to revolt, that is to say, one for whom one can die.

Meditations on Yossel Rakover

꙯

Rudolf Krämer-Badoni

Yossel Rakover!

I have just read the letter which, twelve years ago, with death waiting for you to finish it, you wrote to God.

How great must your soul have been, that in such an hour it showed no sign of faltering, but instead was able to utter words of strength and wisdom to your God. And how great must your God be, who undertakes to awaken such souls in man. You belong to the people of God, a people who at all times, before anything else and no matter what happens to them, know how to find a common language with their Lord.

You were right, Yossel Rakover. There is no greater evidence of your being the chosen people than your sufferings. But no evidence of boundless faith in spite of boundless pain is greater than yours, Yossel Rakover!

I belong to a people to whom you would have been ashamed to belong. You can say: "I would have been ashamed." I have no choice but to say: "I am ashamed!" Why, then, do I laugh and joke and work in spite of my shame and as if I were not ashamed at all? Who are we that we unashamedly continue to complacently inhabit the earth instead of striving, in the face of unavoidable death, to live up to the grave responsibility ordained by God for all of us? Only God knows how and why He made us the way we are; why some people die ashamed of being men, and others are ashamed to belong to a certain group of men, but continue to live as if they were not in the least ashamed. But I too am one of those whom you referred to as thieves, Yossel Rakover. I was not one of the fearless robbers and murderers at whom you fired in the ghetto of Warsaw and upon whom you would rather see God bestowing His mercy than upon the thieves—the thieves who, in addition to other evil, were also guilty of the inexcusable crime of fearing man. Yes, I had compassion for the drowning! I hated the robbers and I continue to hate them with all the fibers of my heart. But I admit that in spite of this, because of fear and because I desired to live, I wore their insignia and their uniform. I hated Satan but entered into a pact with him. Something new has been happening to us, Yossel Rakover; the hater came to terms with the one he hated in order to save his skin. I saw train-loads of Jews about to be deported, and I covered my mouth with my hand lest I scream. I was received like a son by a Jewish family in Hungary, but I did not use my gun when the Nazis came to take them away. I saw how little Mr. Strauss in Geinsen-heim on the Rhine was dragged off to be thrown in the gutter; and ashamed, wrathful, yet cowardly silent, I passed him by. Never more, as long as I live, shall I be able to free myself from this feeling of shame. The life which I live is a stolen life now, and yet I laugh and I joke as if I were not a thief! That the robber deserves more of God's mercy than the thief, that is certainly the profoundest word of the Torah that came to your mind in the hour of your death. Jesus, whom your people called Rabbi Joshua, always preferred the outcasts to those who chose to lin-ger in the middle ground between good and evil, always enter-taining the treacherous hope that they would get away with everything. How right he was! I have faith in his words though I don't follow his ways. I may not fool myself with the treacherous hope that I will get away with what we and I did; I hope for nothing but unmerited mercy, but what do I do in myself, by myself, and for myself in order to deserve it? God's ways with

men are as inexplicable to me in my shame as they were to you
in your death throes, Yossel Rakover. We cannot follow you when
you raise your voice against God, when you accuse and demand
explanations. The meaning of your words can be conceived only
by one who loved God as you did. That is what Clemens Bren-
tano's "slave out of the depths" shrieked to God: "Lord, O
Lord! I can't take it any more! Let Your rainbow appear! . . .
Lord, I demand it of You—save! . . . Can't you forgive your slave
for daring to speak to You like that?" But what was left to you,
Yossel Rakover, in your holy despair, is the same as what is left
to us in our burning shame, namely, to keep on trusting in Him
even when all earthly hope is gone. All that is left for us to do in
our despair is to raise our voices and scream, or maybe to try to
drown our despair in an even louder cry of praise to the Lord.
There were murderers amongst us—I am sure you know this,
Yossel Rakover—who died like saints, accompanied into eternity
by a forgiving God. But isn't it possible that even a wretched
thief, yearning for a spark of your greatness, or at least for the
fearless soul of a murderer, might ultimately find mercy in
God's eyes? This is the only hope which is left to those who
under the cover of silence and the mask of darkness succeeded
in stealing their lives from Satan's hand. It is my unmerited
hope, anyway.

A people of murderers and silent cowards; a people of brave
soldiers but cowardly citizens; a people longing for faith but piti-
fully lacking in love. That is what we are! The few among us who
withstood Satan's onslaught, and were killed or imprisoned,
cannot possibly make up for the crime of our silence, the silence
of our vast majority; on the contrary, it makes our crime only
weigh heavier upon us. We are now on trial. The court is in permanent session. We stand before it with devastated hearts, living
our stolen lives. I may not speak for all my people. I don't even
know whether there are peoples or individuals that count before
God. I don't accuse anybody. I have no right to. The only right I
have is to accuse myself. To accuse myself in order to wait and
see whether the Eternal shows mercy to my soul. Woe, if anyone

should construe these words of mine as literature! Our men of
letters have already succeeded in proving to themselves and to
others that they had nothing in common with the murderers,
that the murderers were "the others"; "the others," always "the
others"! . . . But all our words, all our self-acquitting big words
collapse like houses of cards before our inner gaze. So here I
stand, innocent before the law of the world, but with an overbur-
dened conscience, with a burning shame in my heart, and, quite
often, with tears in my eyes. Yes, here I stand, doing my daily
work and sometimes even joking and laughing; and your curse,
Yossel Rakover, weighs upon me as on one who was neither a
murderer nor a saint! There are no deeds that I can point at and
that can speak in my favor, and there is nothing I can say in my
own defense, except, perhaps, that I hope—oh, let us all hope!—
that God's mercy is more real than our weaknesses, than our
plagued wisdom, than our smashed self-righteousness.

Second Meditation on Yossel Rakover

🕆

Sebastian Muller

Half a year ago, Yossel Rakover, I read your letter to God for the first time. Subsequently I reread it several times, and in the last few days I have read it again. Since I belong to the people of your murderers, I feel that I must take a stand on what you say. Rudolf Krämer-Badoni did so in his own way. What he said about himself is also true of me. It is true that we are ashamed of what happened, and, nonetheless, that we live as if nothing happened. I, too, was not one of the robbers and murderers, but one of the thieves. I was one of the thieves who hated the murderers but were too cowardly in their silence to think about anything else but their own skins. And that is how it happened that I, like many surviving thieves, am still alive. I am still alive, but there is a place in my heart which is dead, utterly and irreparably destroyed. I don't know what to call this place. Maybe it is the cell, the seed which alone enables men to say yes or no: a place which is central in me, completely internal, and commands yes and no to my heart, my mind, my hands. I say this only for myself, though there must be many among my people who realize by now that in their hearts, too, this place is, and will continue to be, paralyzed. How else could we explain why we behaved like thieves, stealthily watching the play of the murderers? There are times when it seems to me

37

that there is nothing I would want more than a drop of Jewish blood in my veins. Do you understand me, Yossel Rakover? I long to be your brother and a brother of your people. A few of my friends know about this "complex," for it is what people today conveniently refer to as a complex. The story may bore you, Yossel Rakover, but I feel in me a great need to tell you how I came to this wishful thinking.

Like Rudolf Krämer-Badoni, I am a Christian, baptized as a Catholic. What does this mean? Not very much. I was neither Christian nor Catholic when the murderers were in power. But it is precisely because of the reign of the murderers and their downfall that I now hope that I am on the right path to becoming a Christian. I hope to become a Christian, Yossel Rakover, and I say this to you, because I cannot become a Jew! I don't belong to your chosen people; even if I were to convert, I would still remain a stranger among your own. There is only one possibility left to me: to become a Christian!

Jesus was flesh of your flesh and blood of your blood. I am not one of those who say that the Jews crucified Jesus. Jesus had to be crucified because your God so willed. That is my belief. Listen to me, Yossel Rakover! I believe that your God is the same God we pray to: the God who created heaven and earth, who rules His creation, who has chosen your people from amongst all the families of the earth and made it His own. And because I believe in this God of yours, the God of Abraham, Isaac, and Moses, I also believe that your people are the chosen ones, the people of God, to whom nobody can belong but those who claim direct descent from Abraham. That is why I believe that only you and your people can talk to God on an equal footing. That is also why I believe that only you and your people can argue with Him. It is only your people that were chosen to manifest the devotion of an Abraham to your God and to sound the lamentations of a Job in His ears.

I am telling you all this, Yossel Rakover, in order to make you realize why I am obsessed with the complex of wanting a drop of your blood in my veins; it is because of my love for your God and because of my yearning for the power of your faith. It is for Christians that "no one comes to the father except through the son." That is our destiny. We do not belong to your old bond with the Almighty. We are part of the new bond, and our only hope for God's mercy is through the intermediacy of His son. It is only by dying to atone for the sins of mankind—and He died with the courage so typical of His people, which is also your people—that He enabled those who do not belong to the chosen people to find a way of their own to your God. That, Yossel Rakover, is what separates us from the bond of your people. To you God spoke directly, and thus His word remains imbedded in you forever. That is what makes your people and your blood indestructible to the last day.

My people, however, in my own days, exterminated millions of your people with all the cruelty which man is capable of. I know that your God, who also became our God through Jesus, will not leave our deeds unpunished. It may not happen today or tomorrow, but God's vengeance is bound to come. We, the people of your executioners, may be doomed to go under along with the other peoples who tried to destroy you. But you must realize, Yossel Rakover, that there is nothing I can contribute to that final punishment. I am not even in a position to take direct revenge on your people's murderers, once identified. I am condemned to live as a German no matter how ashamed I am to call myself by that name. I could have left this country and gone somewhere else, as your people so often did when they left the lands of their tormentors behind them and went to other lands. I could have become an American, a Canadian, or something of the kind. Many of my people left Germany because of shame, because they did not want to belong to a people of murderers. (I don't include those who left my exposed country because of fear of a new war.) But I cannot do so yet. Do you understand me? Not yet! Because if I want to stand up before your and my God and seek His mercy, I have to do here and now the things that must be done. I cannot pour gasoline out the window when I see your murderers passing by in the street before my very eyes—

and there are still some who pass, boasting and bragging of being your murderers!—I don't fight them as you did in the Warsaw Ghetto. But the only thing I can do for the final downfall of the murderers of God's chosen people is to become a Christian myself.

This may not be the holy vengeance that you speak of, Yossel Rakover. Those who do not belong to your chosen people, even the thieves, can only hope and pray for mercy. And that is the only thing I can now do for you, for your people, and for my own hope of divine guidance. That, too, is the only contribution I can make to the punishment and downfall of the murderers, no matter how long it may be before punishment strikes. But by doing so, I am bringing nearer the day when every descendant of those who murdered you will recognize but one life and one identity: that of being a Christian, a follower of Jesus. For only He can lead to your and my God all those who are not chosen as you and your people are!

Forgive me, Yossel Rakover, for taxing your patience so much. A drop of your blood, a spark of your faith, a grain of your love of God is enough to give one strength for the day when we shall all face the same Maker. All that is left for me to do is to become a Christian and, as such, to help my people eradicate every vestige of the thoughts and deeds of your murderers, and thus embark upon the only course left open to us: that of Christ. Without Him, we robbers and thieves will never find our way to God—Your God and our Judge through all eternity.

My Encounter with Yossel Rakover

✤

Frans Jozef van Beeck, S.J.

My first encounter with "Yossel Rakover" was only indirect, but
very unsettling nonetheless. The year was 1969. I was in my late
thirties, and, academically speaking, I had behind me three years
of philosophical study, five years of theological study, and six
years of doctoral study, the latter in English and Italian literature
at the University of Amsterdam. In the late summer of 1968 I had
arrived, as a visiting lecturer, at Boston College, to teach, not
English, but theology. For, under the influence of Vatican II, a
deep-seated taste for things divine in me had blossomed into a
passion for theology; and, since faith is both deep and wide (that
is, both liturgical and ecumenical), true prayer and transparent
(or at least open) human relationships were becoming my themes.
I had come to regard the two as both fully actualized and fully
reconciled in Jesus Christ, who (as I had understood in a flash of
blinding insight in the early afternoon of Thursday, December 12,
1968) is at once humanity's wholly transparent, distortionless
window opening out onto the living, invisible God, and the living,

---

Frans Jozef van Beeck, S.J. is John Cardinal Cody Professor of Theology at Loyola University, Chicago.

41

window opening out onto the living, invisible God, and the living, invisible God's transparent, wholly human welcome extended to all human beings, at the expense of none—a welcome that includes the whole world.

A friend in the Netherlands sent me a present: a collection of essays entitled *Het menselijk gelaat* ("The Human Face") by Emmanuel Levinas, translated into Dutch and clarified by means of illuminating notes by Adriaan Peperzak, now happily my colleague in the philosophy department at Loyola University, Chicago.[1] Having tried Levinas's *Totalité et infinité* seven years before, I was vaguely familiar with some of his themes. I especially remembered his insistence that more than anywhere else, it is in the face of *the other* that we meet the unconditional demand for goodness, thoughtfulness, and concern that lies at the heart of the moral (that is, the responsible) life; before morality ever wells up from the depth of our autonomy, Levinas had long insisted, it arises in us in response to a call from outside. I advanced from essay to essay—an interesting introductory tour of a thought-world which, at this early stage, appealed to me mainly because it was reminiscent of Martin Buber's *I and Thou.* That profound little book, which I had read seventeen years before, when I was in my twenty-third year, had not only made me a firm (if largely inarticulate) convert to personalism; it had also occasioned a deep desire in me, amounting to an intellectual conversion. *That* was how I would love to be able to think! To have real thoughts and insights, as well as encounters with intellectually and personally significant others to learn them from and share them with!

Levinas's touch, I found, was harsher, more insistent than Buber's; he sounded much less contemplative and serene, and, frankly, much less religiously comforting as well. Going from essay to essay, I came upon a piece entitled "To Love the Torah

---

1. *Het menselijk gelaat: Essays van Emmanuel Levinas* (Utrecht: Uitgeverij Ambo, 1969).

More Than God."[2] It was, in Levinas's own words, a commentary on

> a text which is both beautiful and real, as real as only fiction can be. An anonymous author published it in an Israeli journal; it was translated for *La terre retrouvée*, the Zionist paper in Paris, under the title "Yossel, son of Yossel [sic] Rakover of Tarnopol, speaks to God," by Mr. Arnold Mandel, who, it would appear, had read it with deep emotion. The text deserves even more. It conveys an intellectual attitude that reflects something better than the reading habits of intellectuals. . . . What this text provides is Jewish learning modestly understated, yet full of assurance; it represents a deep, authentic experience of the spiritual life.

Now, twenty-five years later, what I most vividly remember is the consternation that invaded me as I read Levinas's short, squarely polemical piece—originally a radio talk broadcast from Paris on Friday, April 29, 1955. Rereading only made things worse. There it was. Right under my nose I had the single most compelling intellectual and moral challenge to my Catholic and Christian faith I had ever experienced.

In the figure of "Yossel Rakover", so Levinas was explaining, we meet the core of Judaism: an ordinary Jew, proud of the faith of his ancestors, who, in the midst of mindless, criminal, totally undeserved violence inflicted on him, his family, and his people, holds on to his God. He can do so only by holding on to the Torah. For in a world in which God's countenance is entirely veiled, and in which justice has disappeared and humanity has turned savage and merciless, only those who represent what is noble and holy and godlike—that is, who live by the discipline of the Torah—are left to represent the hidden God. In this predicament, faithful Jews are destined to feel the weight of God's responsibility for the world on their own shoulders; naturally,

---

2. French original: "Aimer la Thora plus que Dieu," in *Difficile liberté: Essais sur le judaïsme*, 3rd ed. (Paris: Albin Michel, 1976), pp. 189–93; English translation and commentary in F. J. van Beeck, *Loving the Torah More Than God? Toward a Catholic Appreciation of Judaism* (Chicago: Loyola University Press, 1989), pp. 31–53.

they are also the first victims of the forces of injustice. Thus in Judaism, cultivation of the Torah makes mature moral responsibility for a just world an ineluctable element of life with the God of the Covenant—the God who, while incommensurably greater than humanity and, hence, wholly incomprehensible, freely and graciously elects human beings (not as slaves but) as partners "capable of responding, of turning to their God as creditors and not always as debtors: *that* is truly divine majesty! . . . How vigorous the dialectic by which the equality between God and man is established right at the heart of their incommensurability!"

Thus instructed and shaped and equipped by the Torah for the disciplined, fully responsible life, faithful Jews can proudly (that is, with a deep sense of their privileged position) acknowledge and glorify the living God, even at times when God manifests the divine greatness only by veiling His countenance.

By contrast, Levinas went on to argue, in Christianity, God's free and gracious love of humanity takes the shape, not of a call to discipline, but of reassurance and indulgence. The sinner's utter dependence on the comforts of the Incarnation and the all-atoning death of Jesus, and on the all-forgiving divine clemency implied in both, becomes the center of the faith. But this makes full moral responsibility negotiable; Christians are permitted (and indeed, encouraged) to settle for a morally imperfect world—are not all human beings sinners, justified by God's grace alone? In this way, not only are Christians excused in advance from the full holiness demanded by God; far worse, they can make their moral incompetence the measure of God's majesty and God's demands. Thus they reduce God's majesty to God's ability to forgive human sins; Christians can rest and take comfort in that forgiveness, and settle, by divine warrant, for a world that is less than just. Christianity's complicity with the Holocaust, or at least its ineffectualness in the face of it, Levinas suggests, are there to prove just this point.

So, Levinas warns, instead of thinking of Judaism as the prefiguration of their own superior religion, Christians had better wake up to the fact that the shoe is entirely on the other foot.

Judaism is seasoned religion, professed and practiced from time immemorial "in spirit and truth,"[3] and matured in the furnace of suffering. Christians have an alibi; not only can they invoke the always-readily-available divine mercy as an easement from full moral responsibility for unjust suffering in the world, but by pointing to Jesus, they can even accept unjust suffering as mysteriously meaningful.

Thus, while Christians can settle for an immature variety of both religion and humanism, Judaism is "an integral and austere humanism, coupled with difficult worship! And from the other point of view, a worship that coincides with the exaltation of man." The implication of all this is obvious. Judaism, Levinas points out, is a religion of adults;[4] Christianity is, in the last analysis, a children's religion.

Despite this frontal attack on my fundamental convictions, I found Levinas's piece irresistible. Here I was, a graduate of the secularization and death-of-God theologies of the sixties, profoundly convinced that faith in God was not a crutch, that we modern Christians had "come of age," and that if any god was dead, it was not the living, true God, but only "the problem-solver God," "the god of the gaps"—the god who (it had been thought) was needed to fill the lacunae still left in the human understanding of the world and humanity, and to provide irresolute, immature believers with the props they still needed. The central contention of Levinas's essay blew this complacent theological picture of myself and my theological generation out of the water. For what Levinas was equivalently saying was this: precisely because the God of the Christians is the God of the Incarnation, of the close comfort involved in a humanity shared with God, and of unconditional indulgence and forgiveness extended to human weakness for the sake of Jesus' Passion and death, the Christian God *is* the god of the gaps *par excellence*. Christianity, in other words, draws the living God into complic-

3. Obviously, this is a quotation from the Gospel of John (4:25).
4. Cf. "Une religion d'adultes," in *Difficile liberté*, pp. 24–41.

ity with human injustice, interpreted as an acceptable part of the world. With a terrible clarity I saw that I must come to terms with this piece if I wanted to be a Christian, a Catholic, a Jesuit, a priest with intellectual and moral integrity. Thank heavens I also realized that it would take time. But a great quest had begun.

★ ★ ★

My quest clearly consisted of two parts. First of all, I must begin to think through Levinas's interpretation of Christianity and its relatedness to Judaism. That was the main task and the most demanding by far. Secondly (as well as more practically), I must find the story that Levinas had commented on.

For a start, I tracked down the French original of Levinas' radio broadcast, translated it into English, and, initially with more zeal than discernment, began using it in the christology courses I was teaching. Thus I got to understand it thoroughly— an essential first step if I were ever going to come to terms with it. I also wrote to a Dutch Jesuit friend who was studying in Paris at the time. I asked him to find the "Yossel" story in *La terre retrouvée* and send me a copy. He did. In fact, he not only sent me a clumsy photocopy of the actual pages; he became so engrossed in the French text that he went to the trouble of typing it out for me in full. At the very least, I had more translation work ahead of me.

In the meantime, in January, 1973, before I received the French text, I had temporarily moved to Regis College, Toronto. The move would enable me to get a book on christology under-way; I was to return the favor of the college's hospitality by teaching, that spring semester, the basic christology course at the Toronto School of Theology. Not long after my arrival I met Barry Walfish, a young Jew who had recently become the assistant librarian at Regis College. We started talking occasionally, and one day, in the reading room, I showed him my English translation of Levinas's essay. He glanced at it and told me it looked familiar. An hour later he was sure he knew the story

Levinas was talking about. The next day he came to see me, Albert Friedlander's anthology *Out of the Whirlwind* in hand.[5] I was stunned. The anonymous Yiddish story whose French version I had just asked my friend in Paris to find for me turned out to have an author, in the United States. His name was Zvi Kolitz.

It did not take me long to discover that things were complicated. When the French version of the story arrived, it proved to contain passages that were absent from Friedlander's English version—absent even from the first published English version, which, sometime in early 1974, I had found in Zvi Kolitz's own *Tiger Beneath the Skin,* which had appeared in 1947.[6] This raised questions. What had happened? Who had written what? For the time being, however, these redactional questions stayed on the back burner; I reverted to them only sporadically, as time and interest allowed. The truly burning issue was neither the textual tradition nor the matter of authorship, but the theological challenge implicit in "Yossel Rakover Speaks to God"—the one that Emmanuel Levinas had made so painfully explicit in "To Love the Torah More Than God." However, lest I confuse my present readers by a mixture of theological reflection and reports on my pursuit of matters of text and authorship, let me first tell the story of my involvement with the text of "Yossel Rakover Speaks to God" and its author.

★ ★ ★

By the middle of 1984, I had found—I no longer recall how—a letter that Zvi Kolitz had written, in 1972, to the editor of *Shdemot*, the journal of the Israeli kibbutz movement; Dr. Arye Motzkin, a Jewish colleague in the department of theology at Boston College, translated it for me. In it, Kolitz unequivocally claimed authorship, calling the text "an original story which I

5. *Out of the Whirlwind: A Reader in Holocaust Literature* (New York: Union of American Hebrew Congregations, 1968).
6. *Tiger Beneath the Skin: Stories and Parables of the Years of Death* (New York: Creative Age Press, 1947).

wrote and published about twenty years ago in New York." He further explained that "in 1953, a great Yiddish poet, Abraham Sutzkever, was misled by a Jew from Argentina, who had read the story in Yiddish and passed it on to Sutzkever as a 'document.' Mr. Sutzkever published it as such in *Di Goldene Keyt.*" And Kolitz added: "Meanwhile, the origin of this error has become clear, but errors like these have a life of their own."

In retrospect, it is clear to me that Mr. Kolitz, in this letter to the editor, was appealing to the English text published under his own name in 1947, in *Tiger Beneath the Skin,* solely to document his claim that he truly was the author of the story. At the time, however, I interpreted it differently; I took it as a declaration that the English version was the original, and, consequently, that the Yiddish version behind the French translation was a text that had not only been pirated by an unknown translator, but tampered with as well. That Yiddish version, I assumed, had been sent to Abraham Sutzkever by the nameless Argentinean Jew mentioned in Kolitz's letter. Thus it became a matter of the highest urgency to find the Yiddish version published in 1954 in *Di Goldene Keyt.*[7] When, in late May, 1985, I traveled to Chicago to take up my present position at Loyola University, I had among my papers a Xerox copy of "Yossel Rakover redt tsu Got"; I had finally put my hands on it, in the library at Brandeis University, in March or April, 1985. In the fall of that year, Dr. Anita Abraham transliterated it. In early December, 1985, I finally had everything I needed to start comparing the texts—or so I thought, since I remained unaware of Anna Maria Jokl's German translation published in book form that same year.[8]

However, by that time I had, once again, other things to do; I had come to Chicago to write a multivolume systematic theology. The first volume, started in October, 1985, did not get finished till the late summer of 1987; it was to appear in the spring

---

7. *Di Goldene Keyt* 18 (1954): 102–110.

8. Zvi Kolitz, *Jossel Rackower spricht zu Gott,* unter Mithilfe von David Kohan aus dem Jiddischen übersetzt von Anna Maria Jokl (Neu-Isenburg: Verlag Tiessen, 1985).

of 1989.[9] Work on that book had been intense and I needed a break. In February, 1988, the thought came to me that I might at last be ready to take on "Yossel Rakover Speaks to God"—both its textual problems and Levinas's unsettling interpretation. It turned out that I was ready; by the end of November, 1988, the manuscript was finished. It appeared in the fall of 1989, with an appreciative foreword by my friend Rabbi Eugene B. Borowitz, under the title *Loving the Torah More Than God? Toward a Catholic Appreciation of Judaism.*[10]

In this little book, the first chapter consists of an introduction, followed by the text of "Yossel Rakover Speaks to God"; a commentary on some issues raised by the text brings the chapter to a conclusion. The composition of the first chapter had given me quite a bit of trouble. Throughout, I had operated on the assumption that the text in *Tiger Beneath the Skin* was the original; accordingly, I had concluded that this English text had not only been translated into Yiddish, but had been revised and significantly expanded by one or more alien hands. But Levinas's essay, which was to be the subject of the second chapter of the book, was a commentary *on the expanded text*; in fact, it treated some of the expansions as the most significant parts of the story. If my readers were to make sense of Levinas's argument in the second chapter, they would need to have the expanded text available to them in the first. Thus I decided to print the 1947 English version of "Yossel," but to insert, in indented paragraphs, the seven principal expansions I had found in the Yiddish text, while registering further differences in the footnotes.[11] And by way of explanation I wrote:

> The Yiddish translation . . . had not only dropped Kolitz's name; it had also undergone a process of revision. This is understandable. A story like Kolitz's, appealing, as it does, to such a deeply neural-

9. *God Encountered: A Contemporary Catholic Systematic Theology*, vol. 1, *Understanding the Christian Faith* (San Francisco: Harper & Row, 1989).

10. Chicago: Loyola University Press, 1989.

11. Cf. *Loving the Torah More Than God?*, pp. 13–26.

gic theme as the Holocaust, is likely to elicit passionate responses, and hence, it will invite commentary. That is to say, at the hands of an editor, it will invite editorializing, and at the hands of a translator, it will invite expansion. Not surprisingly, therefore, the Yiddish version shows both: the anonymous translator availed himself of his freedom in order to introduce seven major expansions as well as a large number of relatively small changes.[12]

In putting together this expanded version—the English text from *Tiger Beneath the Skin* augmented by seven passages from the Yiddish version in *Di Goldene Keyt*—I received considerable help from my friend and colleague Jeffrey V. Mallow, who had learned Yiddish in the Yiddish school system, and subsequently earned a bachelor's degree in Jewish literature. Little did I know that in a few years we would be collaborating again. Even less did I realize that in putting together the expanded version of "Yossel Rakover Speaks to God," we were unwittingly approximating, as closely as the data available to us at the time permitted, a complete English translation of a Yiddish text written in 1946 by no one but Zvi Kolitz himself!

This realization did not dawn on me till several years later. It started when, on February 10, 1993, a German journalist named Paul Badde contacted me both by phone and by fax. He had found the Yossel story in Anna Maria Jokl's version, had been deeply touched by it, and had come to New York City to interview Zvi Kolitz. At the end of the conversation, he told me, Mr. Kolitz had given him a copy of my *Loving the Torah More Than God?* When Herr Badde started to read it, he had been surprised to discover that the story existed in several different versions. From then on, it had become imperative for him to try and recover the Yiddish original, which was the reason why he called me. At this first contact, the only thing I could put at Mr. Badde's disposal was my transliterated version of the text that had appeared in *Di Goldene Keyt*. But I did suggest to him that he might call the Jesuit theological college in Buenos Aires. By a

---

12. Ibid., pp. 10–11.

stroke of good fortune, when he did so on March 9, it was Father Oscar Lateur, S.J., the librarian of the Colegio del Salvador, who answered the phone. It was the same Father Lateur who succeeded in finding the text a few days later, in the library of the Asociación Mutualista Israelita Argentina, in the Tuesday, September 25, 1946 issue of *Di Yidishe Tsaytung* (also known as *El Diario Israelita*). On March 12, he hastily sent a pale fax copy of the first three pages of text to Mr. Badde. They established, beyond the shadow of a doubt, the place and date of the story's original appearance as well as Zvi Kolitz's authorship. This was sufficient to enable Paul Badde, a few weeks later, In the *Frankfurter Allgemeine Magazin* of April 23, 1993, to publish an almost complete German translation of the story based on the Yiddish, along with a moving feature article on Zvi Kolitz. In due course. Father Lateur succeeded in procuring a better, far more legible copy of the text as it had appeared in *Di Yidishe Tsaytung*. Paul Badde sent me a copy of that on August 31, 1993. At long last Jeffrey Mallow and I were in a position to prepare an English translation that would do justice to what we now knew was the Yiddish original written by Zvi Kolitz in Buenos Aires in 1946.

We started slowly and carefully. In the fall of 1993 we made a detailed comparison between the anonymous Yiddish version published in *Di Goldene Keyt* and the text in *Di Yidishe Tsaytung*. The first thing we discovered was that what I had taken to be expansions were all part of the original text written by Zvi Kolitz himself. It also became clear that this original Yiddish text, by the time it had been rendered anonymous and before it saw the light in *Di Goldene Keyt*, had been subjected to editorial revision. While most of these revisions were lexical and stylistic, in as many as five places they involved simplifications and omissions. Yet in the end, none of the revisions, numerous and sometimes drastic as they were, substantially altered either the tone or the tenor of the piece. It became clear that either the unknown person who first sent the text to Abraham Sutzkever, or the Yiddishist Sutzkever himself, or perhaps both, had fundamentally respected the text.

By now, the conclusion was obvious: in very different ways and to very different degrees, neither the English version published in 1947 in *Tiger Beneath the Skin* nor the Yiddish version published in 1954 in *Di Goldene Keyt* was completely faithful to what young Zvi Kolitz had written for *Di Yidishe Tsaytung* in his room in the City Hotel in Buenos Aires, in the late summer of 1946.

A story that commands such a wide appeal in North America, Jeffry Mallow and I thought, deserved a better English translation. So, with the encouragement of Mr. Kolitz, with whom I had meanwhile had a moving encounter in his New York City apartment on Sunday, April 10, 1990, we started work on a new English translation. We finished it in the middle of May, 1994; it first saw the light in early November, in *Cross Currents*, the journal of the Association for Religion and Intellectual Life.[13] At long last, English readers were in a position to read what Kolitz had written. A month earlier, the original story had been made available to German readers by Paul Badde, in the form of a handsome little book published in October, 1994.[14] But ominously, on July 18, 1994, the AMIA Jewish community center in Buenos Aires, in whose library collection the original of the "Yossel" story had been found in March, 1993, was almost entirely destroyed by a terrorist's bomb.

* * *

With the issues of text and authorship recounted, I must now turn to the more important questions of faith and theology. What has my encounter with Yossel, son of David Rakover of Tarnopol, taught me?

A first answer must be: simply itself. A good piece of literature is its own study and its own reward; it shapes us the way friends shape us, especially dear and difficult friends: deeply, if often

13. *"Yossel Rakover's Appeal to God:* A New Translation with Afterword," *Cross Currents* 44 (1994): 362–77.
14. Zvi Kolitz, *Jossel Rakover's Wendung zu Gott,* translated from the Yiddish and edited by Paul Badde (Möhlin and Villingen: Raureif Verlag, 1994).

almost imperceptibly. They affirm and enhance us as persons, they broaden our inner horizons and deepen our capacity for appreciation, understanding, and compassion; thus they prepare us for further encounters, with others yet unknown.

But secondly, and more specifically, in encountering "Yossel Rakover" I encountered the world of living Jewish faith in a manner in which my almost lifelong familiarity with the Jewish Scriptures, and especially with the Book of Psalms, had never quite allowed me to encounter it. One of the tragedies of the West is that Christians and Jews have almost no shared religious, intellectual, and theological traditions other than the Hebrew Bible, which, however, we read in significantly different ways. The frictions between Jews and Gentiles that exercised the Christian communities in the first century and turned into the next-to-definitive estrangement between Christians and Jews in the second, substantially reinforced by the later establishment of Christianity as the religion of the West, fixed a chasm of ignorance, prejudice, and adverse judgment between us. Across such chasms, true calls from faith to faith rarely occur. But they do occur.

* * *

One of my favorite instances of such a call happened just over two centuries ago, when an unconventional Christian theologian took Moses Mendelssohn to task.[15] Johann Georg Hamann is nowadays best remembered for his odd-titled tract *Golgatha und Scheblimini! Von einem Prediger in der Wüsten* ("Golgotha and Sit-at-my-Right! By One Preaching in the Wilderness"), published in 1784.[16] It is a vehement attack on Moses Mendelssohn's *Jerusalem oder über religiöse Macht und Judentum* ("Jerusalem; or,

15. I am here drawing on my essay "Israel's God, the Psalms, and the City of Jerusalem: Life Experience and the Sacrifice of Praise and Prayer," *Horizons* 19 (1992): 219–39.

16. The title alludes to Ps. 110:1, one of the classical christological proof-texts (cf. Mark 12:36 par.; Mark 14:62, 16:19; Matt. 26:64 par.; Luke 22:69; Acts 2:34; cf. also 1 Cor. 15:25, Eph. 1:20; Col. 3:1, Heb. 1:3, 13; 8:1; 10:12–13; 12:2). Text in Johann Georg Hamann, *Sämtliche Werke*, vol. 3, ed. Josef Nadler (Vienna: Thomas-Morus-Presse, im Verlag Herder, 1951), pp. 291–320.

argued that Judaism was entirely compatible both with the spirit of the Enlightenment and with the religious, cultural, and socio-political establishment of late-eighteenth-century Prussia. This thesis utterly dismayed Hamann, so much so that even after *Golgatha und Scheblimini!* was published, he remained restless and dissatisfied with himself. In the end, he decided to raise the alarm once again in a brief tract for general circulation, to be entitled *Entkleidung und Verklärung: Ein fliegender Brief an Niemand, den Kundbaren* ("Denudation and Glorification: A Flying Letter to Nobody, the Well-Known").[17] He never lived to see it in print. In capitulating to political and religious convenience, Hamann felt, Mendelssohn had abandoned the voice of prophecy. He had presented Judaism as a time-honored tradition of ritual and conduct, but one that incorporated nothing substantially new in the way of *truth* or *fact.* In doing so, he had settled for the Enlightenment proposition that the only substantive realities are the timeless, universally acceptable truths always accessible to natural reason. While appearing to honor the Jewish tradition, Mendelssohn had robbed it of any claim to real distinctiveness. Hamann felt that his friend had protested too much; unwilling and unable to prophesy, he had denied the chasm that lay between Judaism and the Enlightenment; at Mendelssohn's hands, Judaism had degenerated into a profession of harmlessness. The record had been misinterpreted, and Hamann felt that he had the duty to point this out, precisely as a Christian. For Scripture treats the most intractable passions and paradoxes as part of the *substance* of the faith of ancient Israel and its inheritor, postexilic Judaism—not as incidental to it. Honesty in reading the Bible demands that we refuse to domesticate the truth. Mendelssohn had forgotten the real Jerusalem. That Jerusalem is not timeless but painfully historical, and hence inseparable from the gift of prophecy and the duty to prophesy; only in this way can it be appreciated as the Vision of

17. Text in Johann Georg Hamann, *Sämtliche Werke,* vol. 3, pp. 348–407.

Peace and the Holy City—the substance of faith, hope, and universal reconciliation.

★ ★ ★

Johann Georg Hamann's outcry, across the chasm that separates Christianity from Judaism, came from the Christian side. In the name of the City of Jerusalem—both its historic glories and its historic sufferings—Hamann called on Judaism not to sell its soul for the conveniences of the Enlightenment.

In my case, the outcry across the chasm came from the Jewish side, in the form of Zvi Kolitz's story and Emmanuel Levinas's commentary on it. In the remainder of this essay, let me give an account of some of the ways I have come to terms with its impact. I shall do so by raising three issues.[18]

★ ★ ★

The first concerns the glory of God. In the name of the victims of the Holocaust and of their faith, "Yossel" calls on Christians not to sell their souls for the conveniences of anthropocentrism. Anthropocentrism yields a version of Christianity that is little more than a clearly revealed divine scheme for the salvation of a humanity mired in sin; it reduces humanity and the created universe to a mere stage on which the salvation of Christians is taking place. This variety of Christianity is mainly a religion of piety and reassurance; it assures sinners of forgiveness, and proclaims, often in deeply moving tones, that the forgiveness of human sin is the paramount wonder of God's gracious love and the principal manifestation of God's greatness. Levinas obviously had encountered the type in Europe; arguably, it is even more widespread in North America.

There is an enormous problem with this interpretation of Christianity. In the phrase of Dietrich Bonhoeffer (who was

---

18. The present essay is a fresh effort to give an account of my thinking. Still, it inevitably contains themes and insights also contained in my earlier, and much fuller, response to "Yossel Rakover" and to Levinas's commentary on it, under the title "God's Love and God's Law," in *Loving the Torah More Than God?*, pp. 55–83.

hanged in Flossenburg on April 9, 1944, for his complicity in a plot to kill Hitler), this version of Christianity "cheapens grace."[19] It allows human beings to take comfort in the assurance that they are in God's good graces at no cost to themselves; they can rely on God's love, and God is welcome to be entirely at their service, weak and sinful as they are. But this indulgent, very intimate God is a caricature of the God of the Covenant— the merciful, faithful, steadfastly loving God who "will by no means clear the guilty" (Exod. 34:7). While graciously forgiving the people of Israel its dreary history of unfaithfulness and sin, this living God never ceases to call his people to worship and to loyalty to the Covenant, by the practice of steadfast, responsible stewardship on behalf of all of humanity and the whole world. Made in the divine image and likeness, those who worship the living God must be the representatives, in time and place, of God's own glory and holiness, which permeate and encompass all times and all places.

A Christian community that merely basks in God's forgiving love will lose the sense of God's transcendent majesty. It will believe not so much in God as in salvation, which it will in due course feel free to define anyway it pleases;[20] thus it will be inclined to absolve itself from any wider responsibility, whether for humanity as a whole or for the cosmos at large. This form of Christianity makes human weakness and sin the measure of God's greatness. It fails to remind Christians that God is immeasurably greater than the forgiveness of human sin can communicate and convey. Thus it also loses the ability to remind Christians that God's graciousness is not cheap but (again in Bonhoeffer's words) *costly*: God's mercy should lead the human conscience to heroic, self-sacrificing virtue.

Let me put this first theme in the stark language of theology. Doxology should govern soteriology, not the other way round.

---

19. Cf. his *The Cost of Discipleship* (New York: Macmillan, 1963), pp. 43–114.
20. On this tendency, cf. John Henry Newman's devastating critique in *Essays Critical and Historical*, 4th ed., vol. 1 (London: Basic Montague Pickering, 1877), esp. pp. 47–48.

Faith and theology understood as human participation in the everlasting, worshipful glorification of the living, evermore transcendent God should be accorded pride of place over faith and theology understood as the human experience of salvation in history. Only in this way can the radical asymmetry be upheld that prevails between God and all things created, which is the central conviction of the great tradition of faith in the One True God, both in Judaism and in Christianity. In Zvi Kolitz's story, Yossel's final words combine a profession of this faith in the One True God with that ultimate act of worship, the unconditional abandonment of self, by which human beings acknowledge that God alone is God and that they themselves are entirely God's.

It is only fair to observe that the mainstream Christian traditions of East and West, especially in their great liturgies, have consistently said "Amen" to this ultimate act of worship. In that sense, Levinas's description of Christianity is only partly accurate. Consequently, his comparison between Judaism at its noblest and Christianity at its cheapest must be called somewhat unfair. But the indubitable power of his essay lies in its critical analysis of a type of Christianity which is dangerous, both theologically and morally, yet into which Christians slip only too often and too widely, even if largely unintentionally.

★ ★ ★

The second theme, it seems to me, must be the Torah—God's Word and the exalted repository of God's eternal wisdom. Here both Zvi Kolitz and Emmanuel Levinas have simply forced me to come to terms with the continuing meaning of Torah for Christianity. After much reflection and some study I have come to the conclusion that when the Fourth Gospel declares that "the Word was made flesh" (John 1:14), it brings into play "a number of the religious currents of the time," among them speculations current in Hellenistic Judaism.[21] But one of the themes indubitably also brought into play is the Christian interpretation

---

21. Thomas H. Tobin, "The Prologue of John and Hellenistic Jewish Speculation," *Catholic Biblical Quarterly* 52 (1990): 252–69; quotation, p. 252.

of Jesus' life and death as the fulfillment of the Wisdom of the Torah, so much so that one title that can be responsibly applied to the person of Jesus is "the Wisdom of God" (1 Cor. 1:24), and in that sense, "the Torah Incarnate."

I realize, of course, that putting things this way raises a host of issues between Jews and Christians—far more than can be discussed here. To mention just one: In the eyes of a Jew, what is left of the Torah when, with appeals to Jesus and to the evangelization of the Gentiles, the observance of the Sabbath, circumcision, and the purity regulations are abolished, as the Christian community has done? Christian universalism, while not wholly alien to the later writings in the Jewish Bible, sacrifices far too many essentials of the Torah to be still recognizable as a legitimate form of life in obedience to it.

Yet, it seems to me, there is a bridge across the chasm even here. For Jews, faith in God is as inseparable from obedience to the Torah as faith in God is inseparable from faith in Jesus for Christians; in both cases, the latter is the shape and the actuality of the former (as well as its verification). And, most importantly, *both the Torah and the person of Jesus involve demands of divine origin*. Here Christians, and perhaps Jews as well, have a great deal to ponder and learn.

When we Christians say that Jesus suffered and died "for us," what do we mean? Do we mean that the world was redeemed by a heavenly transaction which occurred without our involvement and from which we benefit without our consent? No. That would be nothing but divine whim posturing as mercy. The New Testament never says that Jesus suffered "instead of us," that is, as our stand-in or substitute. Jesus, Christians say, settled the debt humanity owes to God, but he did *not* do so by *excluding* humanity from what *he* did and suffered by way of satisfaction. If God had decided to impute the merits of Jesus' individual suffering and death to us who believe in him, *with no cost to ourselves*, then salvation would be no more than the cancellation, by mere divine fiat and by mere indulgence, of the sins of Christians; but that would imply that God had absolved Christians from any moral responsibility, either for their sins or for their conversion. That would make Christianity a children's religion indeed, as Levinas well saw.

Against this, what the New Testament does say is that Jesus, in living, dying, and rising from the dead, did so "in our behalf" or "for our sake"—that is, as our *representative*. Jesus, living and dying in unconditional self-abandon to his God, freely took on the human predicament out of compassion, to enable and call us to live for God again, in hopeful anticipation of the resurrection of which he himself is the first-fruits.

Thus, *whereas substitution excludes participation, representation invites it; it even demands it.* Jesus's saving work, therefore, does not get anybody off the hook; on the contrary, having been "bought free dearly" (1 Cor. 6:20; cf. 1 Peter 1:18–19), Christians are restored to both freedom and responsibility before God and insistently called to follow Jesus, for the sake of humanity and indeed the whole world. Faith in Jesus, in other words, is vacuous without life in imitation of him. This is why the praise Christians offer to God in Jesus' name *must* take the form of rehearsing the story of Jesus, not only in word, but also in active and patient discipleship.

Not surprisingly, the mainstream Christian tradition has often put this in terms borrowed from the Jewish Scriptures. It has unequivocally rejected the unfortunate (yet widespread) view of Jesus as scapegoat. That view would imply, blasphemously, that God made the punishment of an innocent the precondition for atonement, and that Jesus, therefore, "had to" be dispatched as humanity's substitute, to satisfy the divine demand for retribution. (There are, of course, good reasons for saying that Jesus was scapegoated and victimized, but if we do so we ought to add at once that this was done, not at God's bidding, but by characteristic human injustice.)

What the Christian tradition, in continuity with Judaism, endorses is something quite different. God's blessing rests on the voluntary, willing, patient acceptance of suffering—even undeserved suffering. The Book of Job stands as the prototypical instance of this affirmation, for Jews and Christians alike. Additionally, the Christian tradition has seen the theme reflected in Isaiah's Suffering Servant bearing the sins of many and interceding on behalf of sinners; thus it has regarded Christ as the lamb led to the slaughter (cf. Isa. 53:12, 7; John 1:29; 1 Peter 1:19, 2:19–24, 3:14, 4:13–16; Matt. 5:10). What all of this means is this: there *is* such a thing as the "law of Christ." It calls for a life dedicated to discipleship, which includes the shouldering of others' burdens (Gal. 6:2).

The differences between the fictitious figure of Yossel and the historical person of Jesus of Nazareth are, of course, legion. Yet I wish to suggest respectfully that what I have just explained establishes a deep affinity between them—an affinity, it seems to me, capable of challenging both Christians and Jews. Let me put this differently. Kolitz's story makes the same provocative statement as Marc Chagall's *White Crucifixion*, one of the treasures of the Art Institute in Chicago. In this disturbing painting, the crucified Christ is surrounded by scenes from pogroms: Jews killed, hunted down, and driven away, synagogues burning, Torah scrolls desecrated. To a Jew, this is the world turned upside down: the cross, traditionally the sign and symbol of their persecution, has become the emblem of compassion. But for Christians, too, the tables are turned. In Chagall's painting, far from being the victim of Jewish rejection—as he is depicted even by the Gospels—Jesus is on the victims' side. Naked and exposed, his only covering is a *talith*; in his death, Jesus has become total prayer. He has also become the exemplar of the suffering, rejected Jews who have none but God to commit themselves to. In light of this comparison, is it surprising that in Zvi Kolitz's story, Yossel's last words are identical to Jesus's in the Gospel of Luke: "Into Your hands, O Lord, I commit my spirit" (Ps. 31:6; cf. Luke 23:46)?

In Chagall's painting, by whom is Jesus rejected? The answer, while not explicit, is very much implied: in the persons of the persecuted Jews, Jesus is rejected by the very people who, at least by tradition, acknowledge him as their Savior. How do they reject him? Kolitz's story answers that question very explicitly: those who profess faith in a God whose universal love-commandment Jesus proclaimed have actively inflicted violence on the Jews for close to two thousand years; even more insidiously, there are many self-centered, irresponsible, and apathetic Christians who are passive, silent accomplices of that violence. Here the figure of Yossel turns into a massive challenge to the Christian conscience, testing its willingness to acknowledge that forgiveness of sin and the assurance of eternal life in the name of Jesus have consequences for the Christian community's commitment to the promotion of justice in the world. A Christ believed in but not followed is a stumbling-block, a scandal, not the center of the Christian faith.

★ ★ ★

The third theme. Here I wish to speak rather more personally. If there is one thing Judaism and Christianity have in common, it is that they believe that the fullness of salvation promised by the living God is still outstanding. For all their differences, both Jews and Christians live by hope and desire for the revelation of the Glory in the resurrection of the just; consequently, both live with the realization that salvation is still incomplete. In this interim, Judaism and Christianity are inseparable—tied in with each other dramatically, in mutual tension. For Christians, faith in Jesus as the risen Messiah has not made God's promises to Israel vacuous; much as Judaism opposes the Gospel, it remains God's Beloved, for the gifts God bestows and the calls God issues are irrevocable (Rom. 11:28–29); whatever blessings God may have graciously accomplished in Jesus and in the Christian community, they have not displaced the faith embodied in Judaism.

My encounter with "Yossel Rakover" drove this home to me, and the manner was anything but theoretical; it put my Christian faith on the line. More than I could ever have learned from books, I came to realize that the Christian community is and remains radically dependent, for its faith and its understanding of God, on Israel's faith and its understanding of God. This fact has all too often been obscured by traditional, yet (upon reflection) relatively superficial assumptions and statements about allegedly wholly irreducible differences between Israel's monotheism and Christianity's trinitarian faith, and between Jewish interpretations of Jesus and the Christian acknowledgment of him as the Messiah. In this light I have also come to the conclusion that the common Jewish-Christian understanding of God must remain the yardstick by means of which contemporary Christian theologians take the measure of modern Western civilization, which has been so deeply shaped by Christianity—its triumphs as well as its failures. They must do so both to the extent that the West continues to profess a commitment to some form of monotheism and to the extent that it has settled for, or positively committed itself to, the various atheisms.[22] I wish to suggest that Jewish theologians have an important part to play in this enterprise.

Since "Yossel," these are no longer theoretical truths for me. It is extremely unlikely that I will ever acquire the learning needed to meet Jewish believers on the ground of their own faith-traditions, nor do I expect to meet many Jewish experts on the Christian faith-traditions any time soon. Others will doubtlessly take up these complementary challenges and shed light on the relationship with the authority and mutual respect that come with broad and deep learning. I cannot afford the luxury of waiting till this comes about. I have come to find it impossible to be a Christian (and *a fortiori* a Christian theologian) *now* without having actual ties of worship (mostly implicit), shared manners, and especially mutual instruction with Jewish thinkers and believers *now*. The chasm simply has to be taken on *now*, in full awareness of our considerable mutual ignorance, and hence, in careful faith, patient hope, and thoughtful affection. For in the

---

22. A first attempt at demonstrating these points will be found in my *God Encountered: A Contemporary Catholic Systematic Theology*, volume 2/2, *The Revelation of the Glory: One God, Creator of All That Is* (Collegeville: The Liturgical Press, 1955), §§96–99.

last resort, God alone can raise up true Wisdom in us and among us, by graciously turning not only the Holocaust and its bitter aftermath, but also centuries of alienation and injustice, into blessings. I have been fortunate enough to find such Jewish thinkers and believers. They are friends in God. They have become part of my company as I Walk the Way. And, I am finding out, like Christians, they come in kinds.

To Believe in God "in Spite" of Him

✣

Klaus Berger

Partners in the Discourse

The story by Zvi Kolitz is a major endeavor to speak of the unspeakable, the Nazi attempt to destroy the Jewish people. That the story may not be dealing with the last event of this kind is symbolically manifested by a present-day happening that involved the story: its original text, as far as we know, went up in flames on July 17, 1994 during the bombing of the Jewish center in Buenos Aires, which claimed a hundred lives and many more wounded.

The annihilation of the Jews in the Yossel Rakover story is strictly perceived as an occurrence between Israel and God. It follows in the classical tradition of the meditations and lamentations of the Book of Job or the Eighty-ninth Psalm. Yossel Rakover, the hero and supplicant of the story, is closest to Job.

Our story has this in common with those other well-known testimonies to the mysterious, dark side of the Divinity: that the text is presented as a prayer. As in the aforementioned texts, the prayer is anything but emotional. Rather, it brings to mind Gene-

---

Klaus Berger is Professor of Theology at Heidelberg University.

sis 18, a mixture of petition, accusation, and discussion with God. In this kind of relationship, we are dealing with appeals, demands, principles, and arguments which the supplicant seems to assume will be convincing to God Himself.

The Supplicant's Position vis-à-vis God

The supplicant not only accuses, but calls God to account, as he himself says. God then becomes, as it were, the accused. To turn God into the accused is perhaps the most extreme way to hold on to Him without, however, losing sight for one moment of His being the sole addressee of the afflicted.

The picture of master and slave which we regard as normal in the relationship between God and His people in the Old Testament is resisted here time and again. The supplicant is afflicted, but not enslaved. He does not kiss the rod with which he is smitten. Very often, moreover, he calls God to account. In the biblical tradition, the supplicant appears totally unselfconscious before God. He warns God rather than implores Him. He has to warn Him, among other things, not to overdo His strictness.

Until now, he says, he has always felt himself to be indebted to God. Now the situation has changed: God is also indebted to him; in fact, He stands accused. Yossel Rakover's long prayer is the believer's final warning. He will not have to wait much longer.

Without hesitation, he reproaches God for trying to keep His people away from Him. Does he really see through God, so to speak, or is it, rather, that such accusations are a most desperate kind of holding on to Him?

Theological Principles

God's actions often seem to rival the Torah. The supplicant prefers the Torah, as a way of life, to God's acts. God's acts belong to the realm of "religion"; the chosen are thus the victims. But as far as the Torah is concerned, they are pupils; as such they may argue with God critically and even invoke His own principles against Him.

1. The self-verification of the Torah and its frequent separation from God's historical acts is one of the most noteworthy features of the story. The Torah appears as the Deity's rational, perceptive, and loving side; His acts in history, however, appear as inconceivable and even unacceptable. Is it possible that God Himself does not hold on to His own Torah? If so, what sin has earned such punishment?

The difference from traditional Western Christian theology comes forth here quite clearly. While Christians saw the condemning harshness of the Law as an aspect of God's strictness, they managed to harmonize God's contradictory historical acts (from Augustine to Leibnitz). The Law condemns man to death, thereby determining his fate. God's healing actions to counter this malaise are seen in Western Christian theology as fundamentally positive. The catastrophes of history are merely accidents on the road to a good end.

The consequences of this perception cannot be overlooked, for they prove fatal. Law and order fall into discredit, and by the same token, we Christians, holding on, as we do, to the notion of the preordained harmony of world history, are left without a category in which to fit the manifestly dark side of history. The explanations and excuses of Christian theology, when faced with the very notion of Auschwitz, only bear testimony to this impasse. The mixture of guilt, fear, and superhuman darkness cannot even be expressed before God in words; silence then becomes entwined with one's *own* dark side.

The very opposite transpires in the story by Zvi Kolitz. The supplicant does not give in to a God-is-dead theology, nor does he indulge in moralizing of any kind, as is so frequently the case with Christian theology after Auschwitz. He looks for a definitive, ultimate possibility to find a connection between the historical events and God Almighty. He succeeds in doing so, if only at the price of a separation, so to speak, between the Torah and God's handling of history.

This approach seems more plausible to me than any in the Western Christian tradition. For the expansive aversion to the Law of Christian theologians has no foundation in the New Testament, and an exclusively optimistic perception of history simply does not deserve to be believed.

2. The continuing suffering of Israel can only be construed as a sign of its chosenness. There must be a system behind God's toleration of suffering of such unimaginable proportions. This thought is, in itself, akin to a response to the supplicant: Israel's very pain has rendered it chosen. Inasmuch as God Himself is the Chooser of the chosen—a chosenness indistinguishable from suffering—He Himself is, as it were, implicated in the torment.

Even the torment, however, bespeaks His glory and grandeur. We are dealing here with the old contradiction, as seen by the rabbis, between God's glory, majesty, and power, on the one hand, and God's life-affirming mercy, on the other. The problem is that the glory and grandeur often assume the nature of a torment. God's compassionate outgoingness, by contrast, became real only with the giving of the Torah.

3. The persecution of Israel renders the Torah even more sacred and eternal.

Torment and persecution are such a monstrous injustice that in their sight the holiness and eternity of the Torah shine forth so much the stronger. The very attempt of the heathen to destroy Israel teaches us what man is capable of when he acts without the Torah and without God—namely, of everything.

But all this horrific injustice leaves the Torah untouched, so that it becomes the embodiment on earth of the most sacred and eternal. But on this level, too, the Torah is pitted, as it were, "against" God. It presents eternity as "the mountain of the Lord" of the Psalms; only His most faithful and most chosen deserve to ascend it.

4. Because of the magnitude of the divine test, God must forgive those who have turned away from Him in their despair.

This concerns the less hardy among the chosen who could no longer bear their torment. Retreat, in view of the mindset created by God's acts, or the lack thereof, becomes a kind of chivalrous malfeasance.

5. God cannot possibly be the God of those who perpetrate unspeakable crimes against the living body of Israel. He is, therefore, much more the God of the dead.

Logic: God is the God of someone, as He is the God of Abraham, Isaac, and Jacob. Is He, can He possibly be, the God of the heathen? In view of Israel's torments, may one not suspect that He is no longer the God even of His people? This tormenting question is now being answered: He is the God of the dead, namely, the God of those who wait in eternity, but by no means *for* eternity, for the divine vengeance that will come to pass when He reveals His countenance again.

6. (the reverse of 5) God is, and must be, the God of those who carry within themselves a spark of His greatness, of His goodness.

Here again we are dealing with the Torah. As the sages of the Talmud say, "The Torah is not in heaven," but with people. Not His acts but only His people, the people of His Torah, project a spark of the goodness and light of God Almighty. While God's acts are often dark and tormenting, the clear aspect of His good and luminous side is to be found only in His people Israel.

7. The reason for praising God is radically limited, whether it be what He has caused to transpire (as in the Psalms) or what He tolerates (like the suffering inflicted upon Israel).

His sheer existence, however, remains the sole reason for praising Him. This existence consists of His awesome and terrifying grandeur. Because it is mostly torment that one experiences on the side of God, as was the case with the people of Israel, God seems to stress His transcendent grandeur by allowing the pains of the unfortunate to happen.

8. Argument for His transcendent grandeur: How great must He be if even that which is now taking place fails to impress Him!

The injustice which God tolerates should actually have compelled Him immediately to intervene and avenge Himself on the wicked. The fact that He does not do so can by no means be construed as an argument against Him, but rather as the definitive proof that He has, so to speak, strong nerves, that He does not let Himself be provoked prematurely.

9. The supplicant does not ask God to punish the guilty; they themselves will ultimately devour each other. It is an old topic of apocalyptic and rabbinic exegesis that the evildoers of humanity will ultimately destroy each other in a battle of all against all.

10. Rather, God should condemn those who are silent in the face of murder.

Logic: according to the Bible, the thief is more severely punished than the robber. He who attacks his victim in broad daylight fears neither God nor man. The thief, however, who does his work stealthily, fears people, but not God. His offense is therefore greater.

The murderers of the Jews, Yossel Rakover states, should be dealt with as robbers by the Supreme Judge. Those who were silent, however, should be punished like thieves. The reason is that when silence about the unspeakable prevails, all that is left to the faithful is the Torah, which the silent ones, even more than the murderers, tried to render invalid.

11. God has kept His chosen ones away from Him. It is as if He were doing everything to make it difficult for them to hold on to Him. Despite this attitude of the Divinity, however, the supplicant unwaveringly believes in Him. Belief here means to hold on to God even, as it were, "against" Him. Hence belief is a reaction against God's acts "in spite of Him." Are we not told in the Bible that the fiery prophet Elijah, at a certain critical moment, hurled the reproach against God that He Himself "has turned the hearts" of His people away from Him? This extraordinary dialectic has various aspects.

First, God appears, biblically speaking, as the great Tester, as it is written: "And God tested Abraham." He is, therefore, the One who makes it exceedingly difficult for man to believe in Him. We are dealing here with a test of hardness without comparison, for God is indeed a mighty Tester!

The second aspect: God is engaged, as it were, in waging a battle with His followers. Life, then, is a battle fought around the question whether He will "succeed" in keeping man away from Him. Where God is directly addressed, or where the supplicant is still able to argue with Him, there tormented man no longer appears as a slave of God, but, in a manner quite "modern," as His partner, as one who wrestles with Him, like Jacob of old with the angel. Excessive suffering entitles man to his emancipation. The Old Testament kind of relationship between master and slave emerges out of the crucible of unprecedented horror as somehow suspended.

Third: The question here is no longer of any personal hope for future or rescue whatsoever. Rather, the supplicant gains his honor, his self-worth, his final firm stand vis-à-vis the Divinity, by not letting himself be led astray from God by God! The choice then becomes an end in itself, for suffering, mated to the Torah, remains the only sign of chosenness.

Fourth: He who makes it so difficult to follow Him—as is the case of God versus His chosen ones—seemingly desires to put their love to a "provocative" test. He desires to really know the limits, or limitedness, of their love, as was the case with the almost impossible test to which Abraham was put. That is why the supplicant says in the Rakover story, "I will always love You in spite of Yourself." What the supplicant gains from this experience is this: that He who makes it most difficult for another to follow Him, most desires his love. Love always consists of an element of "in spite of."

Fifth: Whereas in the Torah everything depends upon fulfilling God's will, so, in view of God's acts, everything seems to hinge upon resisting His acts, for they make it exceedingly difficult for man to hold on to Him. Here lies the whole meaning of being in the world—if there is a meaning.

Sixth: "There is nothing more whole than a broken heart."

To belong to the most unfortunate of nations is sheer good fortune for the supplicant. This paradox can be solved by one sentence: God deals harshly with His people because they are

the recipients of His commandments. The result is a specific
kind of openness and revealedness: that of the martyr. For it is
quite clear that when someone must suffer for being the pos-
sessor of the "highest Law" and "most sublime morality," the
injustice against him becomes an insurmountable scandal.

The obvious contrast establishes the supremely impressive
function of martyrdom for all time. Because the martyr, through
his fierce innocence, honors what he is dying for. What is new
here is that God Himself seems to have joined the ranks of those
who create martyrs. He actually presents a living proof for the
truth of the Torah. It infuses the martyr's Torah, which is the
tyrant's nemesis, with a divine light which the supplicant cannot
help but regard as emanating from a "just" and decent God, for
it stands, after all, for the Highest Law and the most perfect
morality.

Vengeance and Self-Worth

There is something to be said about two seeming incongruities
in the Rakover story. Yossel Rakover has an uncomplicated attitude to vengeance and to his own self-worth.

Yossel Rakover, without a trace of moral scruple about vengeance, speaks of the sacredness of retribution and of his profound satisfaction on having consigned a tank full of Nazis to
the flames. At this point the non-Jewish reader should guard
himself against three things: moral judgment or assessment of
that which, even keeping the background of the events in mind,
he is not entitled to judge; the idea that Judaism is a religion of
revenge; and above all, a hypocritical good relationship with
one's own thirst for revenge. Actually, one can learn from this
prayer how to open up before God unsparingly with one's whole
right and wrong. Christian prayer is all too often morally cen-
sored and, hence, untrue and dishonest. In the situation of the
supplicant, joy over vengeance and thirst for divine retribution,
far from being cruel, are downright honest. Contrary to the
"bravery" of our prayers, God appears here as a dialogical part-

ner, for man cannot help but react with his own dark side to the horrors before him.

The other point concerns Yossel Rakover's sense of moral self-worth. The supplicant does not writhe like a sinner before God. Instead he says, "I would like to see how the heathen would have behaved in our place"—a statement which should not be taken as dramatically serious, but rather as betraying a touch of humor and irony, a blink in the midst of a confrontation with God. If this seems inappropriate, one should bear in mind that before God hardly anything is appropriate; in addition, it concerns the collective, not the individual.

* * *

One can be for God, and one can be against Him. But one cannot be without Him.

—Hasidic saying

Holocaust Challenges to Religious Faith: The Cases of Yossel Rakover, Hersh Rasseyner, and Chaim Vilner

✿

Marvin Fox

Serious literature that deals with the human condition necessarily has some philosophical and religious dimensions. This is especially true of the literature of the Holocaust. Even purely historical or documentary treatments of the Holocaust are permeated with philosophical and religious questions. These accounts of human behavior in extreme situations force us to confront questions about what it means to be human. Sober historical descriptions of heroism or degradation, of suffering or redemption, engage us in the effort to understand more than the facts. They force us to consider as well the ultimate significance of these manifestations of what is possible in human behavior.

When poets, short story writers, or novelists use their literary imaginations to reflect on human catastrophe, the religious and philosophical questions are more vivid and more demanding. The

---

Marvin Fox is Philip W. Lown Professor of Jewish Philosophy Emeritus at Brandeis University.

imaginative writer dealing with Holocaust themes forces his
readers to confront directly the hard and agonizing questions
about the role of God and the response of man in the grotesque
world in which European Jewry was destroyed. Whether the
confrontations with these themes are explicit or not, they are
present, at the very least, as an undercurrent which informs the
literary work and gives it a certain philosophical and religious
character. There is no serious Holocaust literature in which
these philosophical and religious concerns are completely
absent.

In this essay we shall consider two short literary works which
emerge from the Holocaust experience, works in which the religious and philosophical concerns are quite explicit. Zvi Kolitz,
in his short story "Yossel Rakover Speaks to God," and Chaim
Grade, in his story/essay "My Quarrel with Hersh Rasseyner,"
provide us with superb instances of how literary artists deal with
some of the religious and philosophical dimensions of the Holocaust.[1] Both works were written in the early postwar years,
reflecting the immediacy and urgency of the unhealed wounds
of the great and terrible experience of destruction. The Rakover
story is written in the form of a documentary account of the last
hours of one of the last survivors of the Warsaw ghetto. It is set
on April 28, 1943, the day of the final liquidation of the ghetto.
It consists of a first-person narration of Rakover's thoughts as he
contemplates the experience of the last years and confronts the
inevitable fact that his life will very soon end.

Grade's work is longer and more complex. It is a kind of
hybrid story/essay which has unmistakable autobiographical elements, as Grade himself has confirmed. The story is not literally

1. Grade's work was first published in Yiddish under the title "Mein Krieg mit
Hersh Rasseyner," in *Yidisher Kemfer,* 32, no. 923 (September 28, 1951). An
abridged English translation by Milton Himmelfarb appeared in E. Greenberg
and I. Howe, eds., *A Treasury of Yiddish Stories* (New York, 1958). Kolitz's work
was first published in Yiddish in 1946 and was translated into English in his *The
Tiger Beneath the Skin* (New York, 1947). For the full details of its strange publication history, see the contributions by P. Badde and F. J. van Beeck in this
volume.

true in the sense that the conversation which it reports took place in the exact form in which it is rendered here. Nor is Rasseyner the actual name of the central figure. However, there was such a type among Grade's friends. He did meet with him on various occasions in Bialystok and Vilna, and did have conversations with him in Paris. We cannot know whether any of those conversations are preserved literally in the story. Even if some of it reflects an actual conversation, it is, of course, embellished and transformed by the literary art of the writer. It reflects reality in the deepest sense, not as a simple stenographic report of a meeting, but as the intense confrontation of the artist/thinker with the profound problems of Jewish existence after the Holocaust. That Grade intended it to be taken as deep history, barely veiled as fiction, is evident from the fact that he himself is unmistakably identified as the person who carries on the long and arduous debate with Hersh Rasseyner. The story begins with two brief prewar episodes in which Chaim (i.e., Grade) confronts Hersh Rasseyner, his former yeshiva colleague. It continues with a meeting in Paris in 1948, where the two old friends come together by chance. Both the Kolitz story and the one by Grade confront critical questions posed by the Holocaust. For Rakover the urgent concern is how to die as a Jew in the face of the horrors he has witnessed and endured. For Grade and Rasseyner the issue is how to continue to live as Jews in a world which has suffered and survived the agonies of the Holocaust.

Three distinct Jewish types are portrayed in these two stories. Rakover identifies himself in his opening words as "a Hasid of the Rabbi of Ger," with all that that implies. Rasseyner is a product of the Novaredok musar yeshivot. It is in this setting that his spiritual and intellectual life was formed, and he has remained firm and fixed in the style of life and thought which he learned there. Grade is partially a product of the same musar education. In addition, he lived and studied privately for seven years with the great talmudic sage, Rabbi Avraham Yeshayahu Karelitz, known as the Hazon-Ish. Despite his deep attachment to the world of the yeshiva, and even more to his saintly teacher, Grade

abandoned traditional faith and observance to become a secular
Yiddish writer. The stories are studies in conflict. Rakover confronts the corrupt world around him and, at the same time, the
God whom he serves faithfully even with his last breath. Grade
and Rasseyner are in conflict with each other, with opposing
ideologies, and with the evil which they have experienced in the
years of the destruction.

Yossel Rakover's Inner Struggle

As we have already noted, Yossel Rakover identifies himself in
the opening line of the story as a Hasid of the Rabbi of Ger. This
is intended to convey to the informed reader a deep awareness of
just what kind of man is being portrayed here. Ger Hasidism is
characterized by its unremitting devotion to learning and the
intellectual life. In this tradition, Rakover proves himself to be
an intensely thoughtful man who, even in the last hours of his
life, engages in reflection on ultimate questions in a way that is
neither maudlin nor sentimental. It is, rather, the way of the disciplined mind, informed by learning, that grapples with the
problem posed by the meaning of his life and of his impending
death. Ger, faithful to its inheritance from the Hasidism of
Kotzk, is also uncompromising in its devotion to truth. No
quarter is given, not even to God, when truth is at stake.[2] In
addition, as might be expected, Ger is based on profound faith
and intense piety. Yossel Rakover, the Gerer Hasid, shows himself in this account of his last hours to be a paradigmatic representative of the Hasidic group that formed him. He is learned
and reflective; he is totally committed to truth; and he is firm in
his faith to the very end.

Rakover begins his reflections with a brief account of how in
the previous period he lost his wife and six children. The world

---

2. For a study of the Kotzker commitment to truth as a supreme value, see
Abraham Joshua Heschel, *A Passion for Truth* (Philadelphia: Jewish Publication
Society, 1973), and his two-volume Yiddish work, *Kotzk: in Gerangl far Emes-
dikeyt* (Tel Aviv, 1973).

in which he lives is a place of unmitigated cruelty. He resents the commonplace comparison of the human oppressors to beasts, because he considers it an insult to the beasts. "It is," he says, "untrue that the tyrant who rules Europe now has something of the beast in him. He is a typical child of modern man; mankind as a whole spawned him and reared him. He is merely the frankest expression of its innermost, most deeply buried instincts." The Gerer Hasid looks at the contemporary world through his Hasidic Jewish eyes and sees in it the ultimate self-degradation of man. Modernity, with its lack of fixed morality, its relativism, its search for self-satisfaction, this modernity is the culprit. It has generated the depraved man who now rules Europe and the depraved society which serves as his instrument for causing the suffering and death of the innocent.

In a bitter confrontation with reality, Yossel Rakover tells of a night in the forest when he met a pathetic dog that was hungry and ill. The two sad creatures huddle together and cry bitterly as they seek to bring some small comfort to each other.

> If I say that I envied the animals at that moment, it would not be remarkable. But what I felt was more than envy. It was shame. I felt ashamed before the dog to be, not a dog, but a man. That is how matters stand. That is the spiritual level to which we have sunk. Life is a tragedy, death a savior; man a calamity, the beast an ideal; the day a horror, the night relief.

This is the state of mind in which Yossel Rakover faces his death. He sees the corruption of the world which he is leaving. He is bereft of all that was dear to him, his wife, his children, his hope and his trust in man's humanity.

Remarkably, his last hours are not a time of bitter recrimination. He finds himself, rather, in a kind of ambivalent conflict with God and in open conflict with the human enemy. As he explores his relationship with God, he is clear about the complaints that he can legitimately raise, but he is unwilling to give up his faith under any circumstances. In his last words he addresses God and says to Him that all His efforts to drive Yossel away are unsuccessful.

> And these are my last words to You, my wrathful God: nothing will avail You in the least. You have done everything to make me renounce You, to make me lose my faith in You, but I die exactly as I have lived, crying: Eternally praised be the God of the dead, the God of vengeance, of truth and of law, Who will soon show His face to the world again and shake its foundations with His almighty voice. Hear, O Israel, the Lord our God, the Lord is One. Into your hands I consign my soul.

In Job-like fashion, Rakover denies that the suffering of the Jews is punishment for their sins, anymore than his personal suffering is to be justified as a consequence of his sinfulness. On the contrary, he knows that he has lived a good, decent, and pious life of devotion to the service of God. He denies that there are any readily available explanations of the terrible catastrophe. One can only say that God has withdrawn from the world, has hidden His face, thereby leaving man free to behave in all his unrestrained cruelty. The effect of God's withdrawal is that mankind has been sacrificed "to its wild instincts." We have no choice but to accept the results of God's removal of Himself from the world, but we may not justify Him at the expense of His people. "For saying that we deserve the blows we have received is to malign ourselves, to desecrate the Holy Name of God's children." In so doing we also malign and desecrate our God.

With these declarations Yossel Rakover has prevailed in his conflict with God. No suffering, no injustice in the world, no level of human corruption will drive him from his faith in God. The Lord of the world with all His omnipotence cannot force this pious Jewish soul to deny Him. This is not to say that Rakover is passive or submissive. He is defiant and demanding. Even while affirming his faith, he also challenges God's action or inaction. He faces the divine majesty with remarkable self-assurance, refusing to bow his head or fold his arms in submission or withdrawal. His affirmation of faith, despite God's efforts to

drive him away, is followed by an uncompromising self-asser-
tion.

> I believe in Your laws even if I cannot excuse Your actions. My rela-
> tionship to you is not the relationship of a slave to a master but
> rather that of a pupil to his teacher. I bow my head before Your
> greatness, but will not kiss the lash with which you strike me. I love
> God, but I love His Torah even more. If I were to discover that I
> was deluding myself about Him, I would continue to observe his
> Torah.

Having thus affirmed himself, he goes on to make a striking
argument that God must truly be the God of the Jewish people.
How could He possibly be the God of the oppressors? "Now I
know that You are my Lord, because after all You are not, You
cannot, after all, be the God of those whose deeds are the most
horrible expressions of ungodliness. If You are not *my* Lord, then
whose Lord are You? The Lord of the murderers?" In this way
Yossel Rakover emerges strong and victorious from his conflict
with God. With a clear eye and a totally realistic perception of
what has happened to European Jewry, he fearlessly confronts
the God of Israel, while remaining absolutely firm in his own
religious faith.

Rakover also is victorious in his conflict with the oppressor.
True, the oppressor can and will take Yossel's life, but all of his
power cannot serve to destroy his spirit or to compromise his
values. He looks at his persecutors with contempt and repug-
nance. All of their effort to degrade the Jews only generates in
Rakover pride and confidence. As he puts it, "I am proud that I
am a Jew not in spite of the world's treatment of us, but precisely
because of that treatment. I should be ashamed to belong to the
people who spawned and raised the criminals who are responsible for the deeds that have been perpetrated against us." His
Jewish pride and his loftiness of spirit remain unbroken despite
all the efforts of the enemy to induce in their victims a feeling of
worthlessness.

He wins his conflict with the enemy not only through the preservation of self-pride and Jewish pride. He wins also at a practical level. In the end he will, of course, lose his life, as have millions of others. However, he is determined to fight actively and to bring down as many of the enemy as possible up to the very last moment. Rakover carries on this battle with an affirmative spirit and with singleness of purpose. Each German that he destroys is one more occasion for satisfaction, one more assertion of his own worth against the corrupt and cruel murderers of the Jewish people. Yossel relates that over the period of the battle in the Warsaw ghetto he exploded scores of bottles of gasoline over the heads of the enemy attackers. And now he has three bottles left, for which he has made careful plans. One will be emptied on himself to facilitate the burning fire in which he knows he is about to die. In this empty bottle he will place this document, his last testament and his message to those who survive. He hopes that it will be found after the struggle has ended and that it will serve to teach the world about "the emotions of a Jew, one of millions, who died forsaken by the God in whom he believed unshakably." The remaining two bottles of gasoline will be used to attack the enemy as they break into the room where he is hiding. In his last moment he still wants the satisfaction of going down fighting and taking with him to death some of his persecutors.

Rakover is in no way apologetic or defensive about his attacks on the enemy. Quite the contrary! He sees this as part of his sacred duty and he carries it out with deep satisfaction. There is for him no morality of turning the other cheek, of seeking to justify or placate the perpetrator. He recognizes unmitigated evil for just what it is, and he is convinced, as a pious Jew, that to fight against that evil is a most honorable and virtuous act. Moreover, he affirms that such attacks on the enemy are and should be accompanied by delight in his downfall. Western culture has often been embarrassed by the desire for vengeance, but not so Yossel Rakover. In discussing the earlier occasions when he blew up bottles of gasoline over the heads of his oppressors, he says:

> It was one of the finest moments in my life when I did this, and I was shaken with laughter by it. I never dreamed that the death of people—even of such enemies—could cause me such great pleasure. Foolish humanists may say what they choose. Vengeance was and always will be the last means of waging battle and the greatest spiritual release of the oppressed. . . . I know now why my heart is so overjoyed at remembering that for thousands of years we have been calling our Lord a God of Vengeance: A God of Vengeance is our Lord. . . . We have had only a few opportunities to witness true vengeance. When we did, however, it was so good, so worthwhile, I felt such profound happiness, so terribly fortunate that it seemed an entire new life was springing up in me.

Here the victory over the oppressor comes to Rakover both by his success in killing some of the enemy and by the vindication he feels in doing so. Here too he, the Gerer Hasid, stands against what he sees as the corruption of modernity. It is a world which preaches love but practices hate; a world which openly deplores vengeance but takes secret satisfaction in the downfall of enemies. Rakover has the strength and honesty to be open about his feelings. He wants his enemies to be destroyed, and he delights in their deaths. In the religious traditions of the Western world it is often held that vengeance belongs to God alone, but Yossel sees himself as doing God's work when he destroys the Nazi persecutors. If God has chosen to be absent, then man must do His work. When man does that work, he is entitled to delight in it and to find satisfaction in his success. Whatever the "foolish humanists" may say about it, for the downtrodden vengeance is "the last means of waging battle." Again, even while death is only minutes away, Yossel triumphs over his enemy.

This is Yossel Rakover. A Gerer Hasid who faces God lovingly, faithfully, but fearlessly. A Jew who, even in the most extreme circumstances, continues to use his learning and his intellect to think through and come to terms with the mystery of Jewish suffering. He remains true to the God of Israel, even when He tries to drive him away. He uses his intelligence to formulate his own account of the absent God. He values truth and will not compromise it by cheap or easy justifications of God. His untainted Jewish pride elevates him above the degraded enemy and thereby grants him the one victory which no power can take from him. His courage helps him to battle against the enemy and to exult in his small successes. He has answered the question of how to die as a Jew in a magnificent and moving way. The inner resources of faith and learning are the instruments which fashion his answer. The courage of true faith gives substance to that answer. Yossel Rakover dies as he lived. He is, to the very end, the man whom he describes in the opening sentence of his testament, "a Hasid of the Rabbi of Ger and a descendant of the great, pious, and righteous families of Rakover and Meisel."

Chaim Vilner and Hersh Rasseyner: A Battle of Searching Spirits

Chaim Grade's "My Quarrel with Hersh Rasseyner" is one of the great achievements of postwar Yiddish literature. Such a work could only have been produced by a literary master deeply rooted in the intellectual, artistic, and religious life of East European Jewry before and after the terrible years of destruction. The author could only be a Jew with profound classical talmudic learning, great philosophical and theological sophistication, and an intense personal experience of the allures and dangers of modern European society. Chaim Grade is one of the very few Yiddish writers with this combination of qualifications. This special background is evident in all of his writing, and particularly in "My Quarrel with Hersh Rasseyner." As we suggested earlier, this story, with all of its autobiographical elements, must be seen as a work of literature which, like all true literature, opens us up to a deeper and more sensitive grasp of reality than that which is possible in straightforward historical prose. Grade reflects on the spiritual struggles of Jews who, having survived the Holocaust, are challenged to work out an answer to the question how one should live as a Jew after the unspeakable suffering of the years of the destruction.

He and his antagonist, Hersh Rasseyner, share a common heritage. They both come from backgrounds of traditional Jewish piety and learning. They were both deeply affected by the life and teaching of the musar yeshivot in which they were educated. Those yeshivot were concerned primarily with building virtuous character. Greater emphasis was placed on virtue than on intellectual achievement. True, learning was not neglected, but it came second to constant self-examination, to discovering and exposing one's own moral flaws. This process of self-discovery and self-transformation tended to become a permanent and inescapable feature of the character of those who had been exposed to it. It was rooted in an attitude of contempt for the secular world, a conviction that what matters most is for man to turn inward so that he may perfect himself. Rasseyner never left the world of the musarists, and he emerged after the war more strongly rooted in it than ever. His years in concentration camps had the effect of deepening his piety and intensifying his contempt for the larger society, including the non-musarist Jewish world.

Chaim,[3] on the other hand, left the musar yeshiva in stages. First he became the private pupil and the personal companion of the great Hazon Ish. From him he learned both a more sophisticated method of talmudic study and a more balanced approach to the demands of musar. His seven years of continuous association with this unique teacher left permanent marks on his soul. One need only read the various elegies that he wrote after the death of the Hazon Ish to see the extent to which even the "emancipated and secularized" Chaim Grade carried in the

---

3. I leave deliberately unresolved the ambiguity of the name "Chaim" as referring both to Chaim Grade, the author, and Chaim Vilner, the character in the story. The overlap between the lives of the author and the fictional character is so great that one can hardly distinguish them. The ambiguity is made stronger when, as we shall soon see, Hersh Rasseyner identifies the Chaim of his conversations as the author of a book of poems carrying the actual title of Grade's first published volume.

depths of his being the image and the teachings of his great master. He mourns his teacher without stop and confronts with great pain his personal failure to live up to the hopes and expectations of the saintly sage. In a moment of anguished confession, as he mourns his departed teacher, he says, "I know that I caused pain to my teacher, because I did not want to remain in the house of God." He concludes this elegy giving expression to the permanence of the influence of the Hazon Ish on his life and thought: "I shine in the reflection of his great love, although he did not want to give his blessing to my way of life."[4] Grade abandoned the house of study to become a Yiddish writer, a member of a literary society characterized largely by its secular humanism. Despite the pathos of his unbroken and unbreakable attachment to the Hazon Ish, he chose to follow an alien path. The Chaim whom we meet in the confrontation with Hersh Rasseyner is a product of more diverse and more complex forces than those which affected his old friend. He too wants to be able to live affirmatively as a Jew even after the horror of the Holocaust, but for him the path is not nearly so straight or so easily formed. The effect of the Hazon Ish on him is permanent. No less permanent is the effect of the years in the musar yeshivot. As Rasseyner says to him in their first meeting, "You surely know what we [musarniks] are accustomed to say: One who has studied musar will never again be capable of enjoying his life."[5] As we study their conflict and confrontation, we will see the effects of the richly textured worlds from which Chaim has emerged, and the tensions which are generated between him and Hersh Rasseyner.

---

4. Chaim Grade, "Elegie oyfn Hazon-Ish," *Die Goldene Keyt* 18 (1954): 5–7.

5. The English translations from "Mein Krieg mit Hersh Rasseyner" are largely my own. I have made free use of the translation of Milton Himmelfarb and have also had the benefit of an unpublished translation of the entire work by Professor Herbert H. Paper of Hebrew Union College—Jewish Institute of Religion. I am grateful to Professor Paper for making this excellent translation available to me, and am equally grateful to Milton Himmelfarb for his pioneering effort. Where I have not followed them entirely, it is because I wanted to emphasize certain details of the text with even greater precision than they brought to it.

The ambivalences with which Grade lived his later life are evident, as we have already seen, in his elegy on the Hazon Ish. We should note that to the very end of his life he was conscious of these ambivalences and the tensions they generated. In an interview late in his life he was asked about this point and replied openly and candidly.

> I know that despite the fact that for two-thirds of my life I have been away from the *bes-medrash* [talmudic study house], and despite the fact that, except for Australia, there is no corner of the earth where I have not been, I am still in the *bes-medrash* and in my hometown, Vilna. Whenever I go out, I go out for only a short time, and I am very angry that I am driven to return at once. I would like to leave Vilna and leave the *bes-medrash*, because I know the world as well as others, perhaps even better. But psychologically, spiritually, whenever I go out, I go a short distance, but invariably I return.[6]

This unbreakable tie to a past with which he seems to have broken is evident throughout Chaim's confrontation with Hersh Rasseyner.

There are two preliminary meetings before the long debate which is the main focus of the story. The first takes place in 1937 when the world of East European Jewry, although threatened, is still intact. Chaim Vilner (like Grade), the published poet, visits Bialystok, where he had earlier been a student in the local musar yeshiva. He returns now as a member of a very different society, a celebrated writer who will lecture and read from his works to an audience far removed from the world of the yeshiva. He meets some of his former fellow students, but feels alienated from them. The center of this first episode, however, is his meeting with Hersh Rasseyner. Here the conflict which will be repeated in other forms is first impressed on the consciousness of the reader.

---

6. Interview with Rabbi William Berkowitz, *Algemeiner Journal*, September 28, 1990. Although published on this date, the interview took place years earlier, since Grade died in 1983.

Chaim meets Rasseyner on the street by chance, although he has been looking for him since arriving in Bialystok. The fact that we are told of his search for Rasseyner makes us aware of the extent to which the connection to the musar world still lives somewhere in the recesses of Chaim's soul. The meeting becomes a bitter exchange. Hersh attacks Chaim for having gone over to the secular humanists, and Chaim counterattacks, taunting Hersh with the charge that he is afraid to look at the world because he might find it irresistible. Hersh accuses Chaim of having left musar society because he is seeking this-worldly pleasures. Chaim replies that he is only seeking truth. Grade's first book of poems was entitled *Yo,* i.e., "Yes." Rasseyner sneers at him, saying that he has heard that Chaim has written a *bichl* (a term that contemptuously dismisses the book as a trivial work of no importance) entitled "Yes." "But," he retorts with fiery anger, " I say to you, no!"

Chaim's response gives expression to the abyss which divides him from his former colleague. It also shows us the ambivalence with which he is struggling even at this early stage of his career. He lashes out at Hersh Rasseyner in self-defense.

> And who told you that I left in order to seek worldly pleasures? I left to search for a truth which you don't have. In fact, I never really went away at all, I just returned to my street—to the street of the butcher shops in Vilna. . . . I have written a book entitled "Yes" and you keep shouting in my face, "No"! You can't understand that I myself say to the world order as it is—No! Yet, at the same time, I force myself also to say—Yes! Because I believe in my street.

Hersh Rasseyner is capable of an absolute and unambiguous yes or no because he has chosen to live in a circumscribed world which leaves him untroubled by doubts or dilemmas. At least so it seems. Chaim, in contrast, has to struggle with the inescapable tensions between the Jewish world that he has chosen to leave and the literary secular-humanist world in which he is trying to find his place. His is a troubled soul, agitated and constantly searching. Rasseyner is only in conflict with the world. Chaim is in constant conflict with himself. In his search for truth he can no longer accept the easy certainties of the musarniks. He is condemned to work on himself as the musarniks do, but in a setting in which intensely opposed forces pull at him. If these problems were so demanding in a European Jewish society which was relatively stable, how much more urgent must they have become in the postwar world in which the pathetic broken remnants of European Jewry were trying to rebuild their lives.

The friends have a second chance meeting in 1939 after the war has already begun. Here too the conflict is joined, however briefly. The major confrontation takes place in 1948, when Hersh and Chaim meet by chance on the Paris Metro. Neither knew that the other had survived, and they are deeply moved to discover that they are both still alive. What follows is a long conversation that begins on the Metro and is continued throughout the day in a famous Paris square. As warm and emotional as is the first moment of meeting, it almost immediately turns into an intense and soul-searching debate. After an exchange of information about where they spent the war years, Hersh turns to Chaim with a soft-spoken but very sharp challenge. It is time, he says to him, for you to start thinking about repentance. Looking with contemptuous amusement at the young couples on the train who are hugging and kissing, he asks Chaim whether he still belongs with them. "Do you still believe in the cruel world?" To which Chaim replies in bitter anger, "And you, Reb Hersh, do you still believe that God's providential care is extended to every individual? . . . Miraculously, Reb Hersh, you were saved, but where is our entire people? And you believe?"

Hersh spent years in a concentration camp, where, we are told, he showed extraordinary heroism and total unconcern for his own safety. He is now the head of a yeshiva in Germany where he teaches youngsters who survived the concentration camps. Like Yossel Rakover his faith has remained firm, even much strengthened. Unlike Rakover, there is in him no spirit of defiance against God, no challenge to Him for being absent when He was most needed. Hersh affirms his unwavering conviction that God's providence is always and everywhere with us. For him life would be impossible without this certainty. The years of suffering and sorrow commit him even more firmly than ever to trust in God and to a life in His service. "How could I bear to live without Him in this murderous world?" he asks. The lines of battle are drawn in these first minutes. For Rasseyner, although the world has changed, he himself refuses to change. He clings with ever greater intensity to the convictions and practices which give his life meaning and hope. Chaim, meanwhile, is still beset by the old conflicts, now intensified by the experience of the loss of family and friends in the years of the Holocaust.

The two old friends leave the Metro at the rue de Rivoli in the Jewish quarter and carry on their conversation near the old Parisian city hall, the Hôtel de Ville. This very setting provides the occasion for the clash of their different worlds. The building is decorated with rows of statues commemorating some of the greatest figures of French culture and history. Hersh looks up at the statues which Chaim is admiring and asks sneeringly who these idols are. He sees no great human achievement here, just stone figures which he classifies with open contempt as *avoide zores*, forbidden idols. Chaim explains who they are and pleads with Hersh to pay attention to the magnificence of the sculpture.

In this phase of the conversation the battle lines are clearly drawn. Although the subject seems peripheral to the main issues which concern them, the debate is symptomatic of their conflicting attitudes and ideologies. Their opposed responses to the statues are a small-scale version of their overall responses to their experiences of the years of the Holocaust. While Rasseyner only sees in the statues graphic evidence of the misplaced values of Western society, Grade sees in them permanent testimony to the greatness of the human spirit which expresses itself in art. He tries without success to open his friend's eyes to the goodness which is reflected in the faces of these great cultural heroes of France, to the special light which shines from their eyes. "You call it idolatry, but I say to you literally, without rhetorical flourishes, that I am moved to tears when I see these sculptures in the parks and squares and galleries of Paris. It is nothing short of a miracle. How could a human being breathe the breath of life into stone?" In an outburst of extraordinary love for the literary artist, Chaim goes on to affirm the unique value of great literature. It deepens and broadens our perceptions and awakens our compassion for man in all his weakness. The writer, says Chaim, helps us to understand the struggle of man to overcome his inner drives. He teaches us to judge "even the most wicked of men, not according to his bare deeds, but rather in accordance with the pain that he suffers in the war he wages with himself and with the whole world because of his passions. You do not justify the wicked man, but you now understand [with sympathy] that he cannot act differently."

Here we see Grade, the writer, speaking in praise of the special worth of art and the artist. The statues give him the opportunity to explain and defend his world, the world that he has chosen over the musar yeshiva, over the tuition of the Hazon Ish, over the *bes-medrash* which formed his own character as well as the character of so many earlier Jewish generations. Rasseyner sees in this choice the corruption of Chaim's soul, a corruption all the more painful because it continues to live in him even after the Holocaust. He finds deeply repulsive the idea that any Jew could still put his trust in the literary and artistic culture of the West. "Shame on you, Chaim, for babbling such idiocy." Our whole Jewish world lies in ruins and you are moved to tears by the so-called beauty of the statues. You say that you learn from the great writer to be sympathetic to the evildoer because he cannot overcome his passions. What kind of art is it that makes you sympathetic to the perpetrator rather than to his victim? "If you choose to make excuses for the absolutely wicked wrongdoer, then to me all your scribbling is a disgusting abomination. Condemn the evildoer! Condemn the glutton and drunkard!

You say he simply can't do otherwise? He must do otherwise! What a fine hymn of praise you have sung to these decadent idols, Chaim Vilner."

Here Western culture itself is put on trial and the issues are sharply drawn. Is there place left for religious faith after the Holocaust? Can a Jew of our generation find hope outside the realm of God's Torah? Is it possible in our age to be a devoted Jew and, at the same time, a devotee of Western art and literature? Is there any ground for morality outside the teachings of the Torah? These are the issues, explicit and implicit, that generate the great debate between Hersh Rasseyner and Chaim Vilner.

Chaim's counterattack is weak and short-lived. He accuses Hersh of turning away from the world because he fears that he cannot resist its temptations. Hersh readily admits to the charge that when he was in the yeshiva he did everything to hide himself from what he perceived as the dangers of the world. He also recognizes that by itself this would not have been enough to build the virtuous character that he sought. Chaim counters that it was childish unreality to think that the methods of the musarists would be effective against human drives, lusts, passions, and desires. As he notes, even the terrible experience of the concentration camps did not transform human character. How much less could this have been achieved by the musar methods of self-examination and self-confrontation. Here Chaim reaffirms his confidence that only the light of art and science has the power to elevate and ennoble the human spirit.

To all of this Hersh Rasseyner responds in a tone more of sorrow than anger. The very idea that any Jew could still put faith in the power of Western culture to transform and purify human character strikes him as painfully blind to reality. True, he says, I made great efforts during my younger years to hide myself from the world so as not to be corrupted by it, but the Germans forced me to face reality with a new perspective and a deeper insight. In a declaration reminiscent of Yossel Rakover, Hersh tells Chaim:

Yes, it is true! All of my youthful years I used to walk with my eyes cast down to the earth so as not to see the world. Along came the German and grabbed hold of me by my Jewish beard, yanked my head up, and ordered me to look him straight in the eye. I was forced to look into his wicked eyes and the eyes of the whole world. And I saw, Chaim, I saw—you know yourself what I saw: everything that we lived through. Now I can look at all the *avoidezores* [idols], I can read all their writings which are abominations, and contemplate all the pleasures of this-worldly life, and none of it will ever tempt me again, because I have come to know the true face of the world. And you still say that I don't know the world and that I have unjustly slandered it. Oy, Reb Chaim, repent! It still is not too late.

Chaim is sobered some by this declaration, but is far from ready to yield. Instead he poses what he considers a key question. Since we admit that all men have free will, why is it that, according to Hersh, the philosophers and artists of the world were not able to become morally good? Indeed, why couldn't all the world make itself good? Here Hersh responds with an insight which was earlier expressed explicitly and eloquently by David Hume, a philosopher whose work could hardly have been known to the musarnik. "Reason," says Hume, "is, and ought to be the slave of the passions, and can never pretend to any other office than to serve and obey them."[7] Hersh makes Hume's point in his own way. He denies that good will alone can ever be sufficient for the acquisition of true virtue, nor can the intellect by itself form man's character. Reason gives us, at best, prudential grounds for seeking to be virtuous, but these grounds are always shifting. Today's prudence may seem like needless self-denial tomorrow. The only sound foundation on which to build a truly good life is God's commandments as taught to us in the Torah. This alone can be a stable ongoing force for human self-

7. David Hume, *A Treatise of Human Nature*, ed. L. A. Selby-Bigge (Oxford, 1888), Book II, "Of the Passions," part III, sec. III, p. 415.

improvement and self-elevation.

> The person who lives with reason alone often inches his way, by his own devices, directly into temptation. He wants to become even more clever. He crawls directly into the fire and is burned up. Aside from the fact that reason cannot help him, it seems to me that it is wildly unreasonable to demand of a person that he should live according to his reason. Reason may tell him that it pays to be good. . . . But if he must be good only because it pays for him, then today it may pay and tomorrow not. . . . If a man has no God, then for what possible reason should he obey the philosopher who tells him to be good? . . . There is only one way out: a person should choose between good and evil only as the Torah chooses for him. The Torah is concerned only with human felicity and knows better what is truly good for man. The Torah is life's only true reality. . . . Even when a man believes that he understands also with his reason how he should behave, he must not at that very moment forget that essentially he behaves so because the Torah commands him.

Rasseyner adds that even the Torah is insufficient if one supposes that he can casually choose to behave according to its precepts. It requires constant working on oneself, constant self-examination, an ongoing effort to form and habituate the will so as to produce a character which embodies and gives continuous expression to the values and the style of life which the Torah demands of us. Chaim's great mistake is to imagine that culture and enlightenment are substitutes for the Torah. Western culture, in reaching its lowest level of degradation during the Holocaust, has shown us the bankruptcy of its supposed attachment to the life of reason. If anyone was unclear about this before the great catastrophe, there is no longer any excuse to continue in this irredeemable error.

For Hersh, as for Yossel Rakover, the opposition between the moral foundations of Judaism and Western culture comes to its sharpest, most unambiguous expression in the Holocaust experience. There one experienced in a way that was almost palpable the meaning of Jewish chosenness over against the moral decay of the West. Secularist Jews are uncomfortable with the idea that

God has chosen the Jewish people to be His representative in the world. Yet, Hersh taunts Chaim, you cannot escape your status and your destiny. However much you may want to cast it off, you cannot remove from your very being your Jewishness in all its force and meaning. Deny your chosenness as much as you like, "you must be chosen, because this is what God wants—notwithstanding you."

In what is perhaps the most moving scene in the entire story, Reb Hersh draws the contrast between himself, the faithful Jew, and his German oppressor. He pictures himself lying on the ground while the German kicks him with his hobnailed boots.

> If at that moment an angel of God would have bent over to me and said into my ear: "Hersh, in an instant I can turn you into the German. I will clothe you in his garments, and give you his murderous face. And he will become—you. Just say the word and the miracle will take place. He will lie in the mud and you will kick him in your—in his bloody face." If the angel asked this of me—do you hear, Chaim? —I would under no circumstance agree. Not even for a single minute would I agree to become him, the German, my torturer. I want the justice of law! I want to take revenge on the criminal! But I want it as a Jew. With God's gracious help I could somehow endure the German's boot on my throat. If, however, I had to pull over my face his mask, his murderous visage, I would have immediately suffocated as from gas. And when the German shouted at me, "You are a slave of slaves!", through my paralyzed lips I said to myself: "You have chosen me."

We need to take careful note of what is being expressed in this moving affirmation. Hersh Rasseyner, the archetypical Jew, will never agree to change places with his oppressor, even in the most extreme circumstances. He seeks justice, even revenge, but only as a Jew. To change places with such a representative of Western culture would be the ultimate act of self-destruction. The depth and grandeur of his Jewish commitment is clearest in the last lines. While the German abuses him as a slave of slaves, the lowest of the low, Hersh mutters to himself, "You have chosen me." Note that he speaks to himself, not to the German.

What the German thinks is totally irrelevant to him. He has no need to impress his persecutor. It would, in any case, be a pointless exercise. He needs only to remind himself who he is, and he does so by affirming that he is one of God's chosen.

Grade makes the point with remarkable sensitivity and elegance when he has Hersh say *baharta bi*, "You have chosen me." The usual formula is "You have chosen us," an expression of a collective special relationship between the Jewish people and God. But Hersh goes further in affirming that this relationship is a reality for every individual Jew qua individual, not just as a member of a nation. You have chosen me. In my hour of agony, I, Hersh Rasseyner, survive and gain strength from my complete faith that I have been chosen by God to serve Him in a special way. That confidence makes it possible for me to endure every torment, because I know who my tormentor is and who I am.

There is here a remarkable similarity to Yossel Rakover, who also wants justice and revenge, but rejects any suggestion that he would be willing to change places with the enemy. We cited earlier his statement, "I am proud that I am a Jew not in spite of the world's treatment of us, but precisely because of this treatment. I should be ashamed to belong to the people who spawned and raised the criminals who are responsible for the deeds that have been perpetrated against us." For those who live within the community of Jewish faith, it is crystal-clear that the worst possible consequence of the Holocaust would be to become like the oppressor, or to become the oppressor.

Hersh has thus challenged Chaim with his own rejection of the world. We must no longer allow ourselves to live in this corrupt world and to be contaminated by it, he argues. We must never forgive and never forget the crimes that were committed and the wickedness which we saw and suffered. To forgive the murderers is to commit the murders all over again. To the question what has changed for him as a result of the Holocaust, Hersh replies that he has become an even greater believer, he feels even more deeply than before trust in the God of Israel, and lives with the conviction that ultimately justice will be done. Without that faith he could not live at all, since it is within the wall of that faith that he has been able to build for himself his separate world. This is what separates and protects him from the moral bankruptcy of Western society. What he wants to know from Chaim is what has changed for him. How can he, after all that they have experienced, still choose to live in this world.

> But you, Chaim, how can you eat and sleep and laugh and dress so elegantly? Don't you first have to come to terms with yourself? How can you push yourself into the world when you know that it lives in companionship with the murderers of your family? You used to think that the world was getting better! But your world has collapsed! Have you learned anything from this, or not?. . . . Where are you? Have you gone forward or backward? What has changed for you? What is your answer?

This is the critical question. Can a Jew, after the Holocaust, still affirm the value and validity of Western culture? Is the way of Hersh Rasseyner the only answer?

In Chaim's response, with all its ambivalences, we see clearly the chasm that separates him from Hersh Rasseyner. His faith in the redeeming power of artistic creativity is as unshaken as Hersh's faith in God. He affirms his Jewishness, but not at the expense of his participation in Western culture. He perceives Hersh's way as the easy way. It disengages itself from all the problems and all the ambiguities of living as a Jew in the contemporary world. For Rasseyner the choice is either/or; he admits no middle ground. But this is only achieved by closing one's eyes to reality. Chaim sees the solution as inclusive rather than exclusive. He wants to bring together in a single cultural framework Jewishness and secularism, *Yidishkeyt* and *Veltishkeyt*. What he seeks is "to find that essence of *Yidishkeyt* and *Veltishkeyt* which can live together."

That essence consists, on both sides, of a genuine concern and respect for the individual, an effort to free the individual to be who and what he truly is. Chaim accuses Hersh of relating to his fellow Jews not as individuals to be prized and loved, but rather as types to be accepted or rejected. He claims that Hersh has no appreciation of the virtues and the moral achievements of non-religious Jews. He does not see their self-sacrifice, their heroism, their martyrdom. Hersh prejudges them all because of their secularism and rejects them as unworthy to bear the name Jew. In his bitterness Chaim goes on to charge that Hersh and his like are responsible for driving these Jews away from the Torah. They closed all the doors to those who were unable or unwilling to meet their own exacting standards. They substituted hate for love and left no place for secular Jews in their framework of true Jewish society. Hersh and those like him are totally blind to the wonderful character of these Jews. They suffer from the blindness of their own ugly prejudice. In fact, they really would prefer to deny that they are Jews at all.

> According to your view, it would appear that the German made an error in taking us [secularists] for Jews. But the truly ugly error is the one that you make. The anti-Semites know very well that we are all the same, and they say so openly. And not only for the anti-Semites are we all the same, but also for the *Ribbono shel Olam* [God]. . . . In the next world your soul will not be covered with a *yarmulke*; you won't be wearing a beard and *peyos*. Your soul will come there completely naked—just like mine.

Clearly it is this conception of the ideology and orientation of the religious community that has driven Chaim away, and it is a conception that continues to live in him and to embitter him. One cannot help but notice the passion with which he has turned on Hersh. In a sense all the ghosts of his youth seem to have been revived.

He sharpens the charges even more when he adds that if Hersh has no capacity to appreciate and to love Jews who are different from him, he is surely incapable of loving and appreciating gentiles, even the most truly virtuous among them. Hersh can only relate to the non-Jewish world by turning away from it with disgust and contempt. But in doing so he is closing his eyes to those saintly gentiles who risked their lives in order to save

Jews. In his world there can be no place for such people, no way to account for them, integrate them, or relate to them, much less admire and reward them. Chaim relates briefly the story of two such elderly gentiles who with complete purity of heart, and for no possible gain, exposed themselves to life-threatening dangers in order to save Jews. Says he to Hersh, "I ask you: where in your world is there a corner for this gray-headed couple? You drive them out into the dark night. . . . The old man and the old woman thought that all of us belong now to one better world, but you spit on that world."

After all these *ad hominem* attacks, Chaim now introduces a serious religious problem. How, after the terrible destruction in which millions of innocent people were tortured and murdered, is it still possible to have faith in God? Chaim considers it an inexcusable deficiency in Hersh that he does not even feel driven to raise the question. The ancients were already concerned about the problem of why the wicked prosper and the righteous suffer. That problem is multiplied a million times over by the million children who were murdered. To say that your faith is even stronger than before while you do not even raise the question of God's justice is monstrous. Although you know in advance that you will receive no answers from heaven, that in no way justifies your not asking. Job and the prophets were no less pious than Hersh Rasseyner, yet they asked the question in sharp and uncompromising ways. A faith which is strengthened by the Holocaust without even confronting the moral and religious problems that the catastrophe poses is a faith to which Chaim is unable to return. He wants to live as a Jew, but his model cannot be that of Hersh Rasseyner.

What is it then that Chaim wants to realize? How does he hope to resolve the conflict? His initial effort is in the final statement of his position as a secular Jew who cherishes both worlds. In baring his soul in these last moments of the conversation, Chaim tries to explain clearly what has changed for him. It is striking that nothing seems to have changed in his dedication to the secular world of art and literature. The only change in his relation to the non-Jewish world is that he will not forgive the monstrous evil which was done. At the same time, he will not permit even that evil to cause him to reject the world. He still sees high value in Western culture, and still hopes for a better world in which we can all live.

What has changed strikingly, by his own admission, is his feeling toward the Jewish religious world which he had abandoned. Despite his harsh language toward his old colleague, Hersh Rasseyner, he now turns to him with a declaration of his love. Chaim assures Hersh that he has never hated him, but does admit that there were tensions and resentments.

> When you became angry with me before I went away from the yeshiva, I also became angry with you. But now I push myself to you with my love. . . . This is what has changed with me and, in general, with all the Yiddish writers. Our love for Jews has become more tender and deeper. That is to say, I do not renounce the world, but I—in fact, I should say—we want to dig up within ourselves the inherited hidden potentialities of the Jewish people, so that we can continue to live. I beg of you: do not deny us our heritage.

Even while affirming this great change which has resulted from the Holocaust experience, this newfound love for his old yeshiva associates, Chaim reaffirms his commitment to the value of the Western world and its culture. No matter how much evil he has seen, he is not prepared to write off or to reject that world to which he is still deeply committed.

Is there then any resolution of the conflicts? Has the long debate led Chaim to any clearer program for how to live as a Jew in the post-Holocaust world? Apparently not. Yossel Rakover, rooted in the tradition, knew how to die as a Jew. Hersh Rasseyner, intensifying his unequivocal commitment of faith, was confident that he now knew even better how to live as a Jew. But Chaim Vilner, who is, of course, Chaim Grade, embraces all the ambivalences of a Jew who loves his people and its traditions, but loves no less the world of art, literature, and culture, which he sees as the core of Western society at its best. As he himself told us, he has never really left the *bes-medrash*, even when he has tried. He goes out into the world, but he is always pulled back. His struggle is to keep both worlds in balance, to remain faithful to apparently conflicting moral, intellectual, and cultural demands. In his final words to Hersh, Chaim reaffirms his love for the Jewish people.

> Don't think, Reb Hersh, that it is easy for us Yiddish writers. It is hard, very hard. The catastrophe befell us all equally. But you have a ready answer for everything, and we have not yet been able to resolve our doubts. Who knows if we ever will. But we serve the Jewish people, even when they turn their back on us. I want you to know that the only happiness which is left to us in our lives is our creative work, and in all the pain of creation we draw closer to our people.

We see here Chaim's unambiguous love for the Jewish people together with all the unresolved ambivalence of what that means for the formation of a life style and a value system. This is reflected in Chaim's final words to Hersh. "I pray that we will both have the good fortune to meet again and see then where we stand [on all these questions]. I pray that I shall be no less committed then to *Yidishkeyt* as I am today. Reb Hersh let us embrace and kiss."

This is the answer to Chaim's dilemma. How shall we live as Jews after the great destruction? Not by a theoretical resolution of theological and moral questions, but simply by one Jew kissing his fellow Jew. For Grade, we can live as Jews in this post-Holocaust world only by embracing and loving our fellow Jews, whoever they may be. Those who reject the culture of the West and those who affirm it, all merit our love and our regard. To the very end, Chaim is determined to live as a Jew by making his world as broad and inclusive as possible, rather than narrow and exclusive. His victory over the Holocaust is just this stance. He will never permit Hitler to drive him away from his fellow Jews, nor will he permit him to drive him out of the world. Whatever the tensions, *Yidishkeyt* and *Veltishkeyt* must be able to live

together. Hersh Rasseyner does not respond to the invitation to
embrace and kiss. We are left only to conjecture what his attitude
is to this passionate invitation to openly love all fellow-Jews,
whatever their relationship to traditional Jewish faith and whatever style of life they may have chosen.

Requiem for a Jealous Boy

✣

Zvi Kolitz

The conclusion of the matter is that in which everything is included.

—*Ecclesiates 12:13*

This is the true story of a boy who at the age of fourteen knew the difference between choosing to die and choosing the time, the place, and the reason for his death. Choosing to die is to commit suicide. Choosing one's own death is to commit oneself to the belief that there is choice even in death, not just in dying. To choose to die is to regard death as an end. To choose one's own death is to regard it as a means to an end that lies beyond it. As Auschwitz stood for discriminate killing—the Jews, after all, were specifically chosen for the Final Solution—I feel compelled to relate the little-known case history of discriminate dying. All those who died in the Shoah died, of course, for the Sanctification of His Name. Their "entitlement," so to speak, to this sacred and eternal state of grace will, however, not be diminished one iota if we stress again what we are all aware of, namely, that they did not choose to die; it was chosen for them. There were, of course, many cases of Jews who chose to die by suicide so as to put an end to their torments. But there were also cases, of which

101

we know so little, alas, of Jews who did not choose to die or to succumb to the death that was chosen for them, but actually chose their own death and insisted upon it as if their very lives— their lives eternal—depended on it.

In a book of rabbinic responsa on the Holocaust, written by the saintly Rabbi Zvi Hirsh Maisels of Vac, Hungary, and titled *Mekadeshei Hashem* ("Sanctifiers of the Name"), I discovered a case history that does not allow for forgetfulness, for it provides us with a glimpse into the awesome secret of the chosenness of the Jews. That glimpse having been provided, of all places, in Auschwitz, it assumes a haunting quality. It haunts us, however, not like a nightmare, but like an illumination; the kind of evanescent and awesome luminosity we sometimes experience at the soundless sight of faraway lightning in the night. . . . Here is the rabbi's story:

★ ★ ★

On the first day of Rosh Hashana [in 1944], when all creatures pass before God like sheep, there was panic and confusion in the camp. The news spread by word of mouth that on that very same evening they would take the boys away to the crematoria. (During the day they did not bring new victims to the ovens, only at night.) In the case of many families in the camp, those boys were their only children, the only survivors left to them. And if these were not their own children, they were children of relatives and dear friends from their hometowns. Such people ran around crazed all day long outside the closed barracks; perhaps a ray of light would appear that would save their beloved child before the sun went down!

But the Kapos paid no attention to their tears and pleas to release this or that boy from among the youngsters condemned to die. As is known, most of the Kapos were wicked and hardhearted men, the dregs of the wicked among our people. Yet in this instance their argument, alas, was somehow "justified." Since they were personally liable for the number of boys they had been ordered to guard, which was an exact number, it would be their personal responsibility to deliver to the SS men in the evening the very same number that had been entrusted to them. If one was missing, they themselves, the Kapos, would be held responsible and would be taken away to be burned—a life for a life.

Even so, it happened that after much effort and frantic pleading and bargaining between the relatives and the Kapos, some of them, succumbing to greed, consented, in exchange for considerable amounts of money, to free this or that boy. But they would immediately snatch another boy from among those they could lay their hands on inside the camp in his place. These were boys who had managed to elude the round-up of the previous day or who had been "freed" during the selection because their heads happened to touch the board.

Now there was a boy in the concentration camp of Auschwitz who was condemned to burn because his head, like those of other youths, did not touch the board. He was almost twenty years old, but short of stature. Because the examination and selection were concluded in such a manner that anyone whose head did not touch the wooden board above was included in the list of the condemned, it inevitably happened that a boy older in years, but small of size, "qualified" for the list; just as a taller boy of fourteen or fifteen could escape the verdict. This young man, Moishele, was a diligent, outstanding, and superior student of Torah, and while attending the Yeshiva of Vac, he had taught Torah to younger boys.

That same afternoon I was approached by a young boy of fourteen from the town of Vac, where I had served as rabbi. His name was Akiba Mann, the son of my dear friend, the pious and highly esteemed Rabbi Baruch Mann, may God avenge his blood, who was the principal of the yeshiva.

The young boy said to me, "Rabbi, what will happen to Moishele?"

I answered him, "What can be done? Is there any way of saving Moishele?"

"Yes," he replied. "I have in my possession enough money to ransom him."

I said to him, "Surely you know that this ransom could take place only at the expense of another boy's life, since the count must be complete. Who can take upon himself the responsibility for giving permission to save him in such a manner?"

He answered that he had a plan for handling this, too.

I asked him, "What plan? Tell me!" He replied with great fervor, "The plan, Rabbi, is that I will go in his place. I take it upon myself with great joy to be sacrificed in his stead."

When I heard this I rebuked him and said, "Certainly, I will not permit you under any circumstances to place yourself in mortal danger, for the Law has long ago determined that one's own life takes precedence." With this he left.

After a while he came back and said to me: "Rabbi, my soul will find no rest if Moishele is burned and I, who am so inferior that I do not even reach the soles of his feet, still walk among the living! I have decided to do it, Rabbi; I will go in his place even without your permission. Promise me only this, Rabbi, that I shall not be considered, God forbid, as one who committed suicide and has thus forfeited his share in the world to come."

I rebuked him even more forcefully, saying, "I cannot promise you even this since you are not permitted to do such a thing. It is very doubtful whether you are permitted to do it under any circumstances whatever. What difference does it make in heaven whether it's you who are sacrificed or him?"

To this he answered in a tear-choked voice: "There surely is a big difference between me and Moishele, Rabbi, for Moishele is a young scholar, brilliant and diligent, and the world will have use for him, but not for someone who is as lowly as I. I am foolish and ignorant, Rabbi, worthless. I have seen with my own eyes the destruction of my family—my parents, my brothers, my sisters, who were led away to be seen no more. In what way am I better than they? What is my life worth now on the face of the earth? But if I can still have the merit of doing one great thing like this by sacrificing my life, which isn't worth much anyway, then perhaps I can save the life of dear Moishele. His life is worth so much more, and the world still needs him. Why shouldn't I gladly and eagerly do such a thing?"

That's how the young boy pleaded with me. I felt that a little more of this precious youth's tearful pleas and my heart would collapse. But I did not give him my consent under any circumstances. After many entreaties and pleas, he left, gravely disappointed.

Now, consider this incident for a brief moment and what was said in heaven about this young boy's plea, which erupted from the innermost depths of his heart in truth, simplicity, and fervor. Surely, he was raised at that moment to the exalted level of the holy ones of old. May their portion be my portion, and may our portion be with his.

★ ★ ★

Ever since I first came across the case history of Akiba Mann, I have been as much haunted by the story itself as by the question of why the saintly Rabbi of Vac, of blessed memory, left it, as it were, unfinished. That Akiba had died as he planned to is, of course, implied in the last words of the rabbi's responsum, "And may our portion be with his." But what prevented the rabbi from spelling out what exactly happened to Akiba that Rosh Hashana day? This I could only imagine: unwilling to say that what Akiba did was a transgression of a sacred law, but unable—emotionally and religiously unable—to disregard the clear-cut case of *kiddush hashem* as manifested in Akiba's sacred yet forbidden deed, the rabbi chose to speak in riddles.

But how, actually, did it all end up? It seems to me that while we can only guess, it is a guess that we may safely call plausible. Enough glimpses into Akiba's pure soul were provided by what the Rabbi of Vac tells us about him—at least for one haunted as I am by the soul of the boy who gave meaning to death at Auschwitz—to imagine how the youthful saint went to meet his Maker:

It was midafternoon when Akiba left the rabbi's side. The initial disappointment soon gave way to a determination so fierce that it supplanted any confusion he may have still harbored with a sense of relief. Akiba lowered himself to the ground, leaning against the brick wall of a blackened barracks, and watched the sun as it charted its course toward another existence. Akiba had to make sure that the sun did not run out on him before he settled things with the Kapo. That was the last thing he had to settle in the world of the living before he went to his voluntarily chosen place in the gas chamber. He was ready for it as for a test—a test he was sure he could pass. Since his family had been separated from him for good—separated with the stunned whimper of captured birds—there was one thing in him that was even fiercer than his grief, and that was his helplessness. Now he no longer felt helpless, not even lonely. It seemed to him now that there was only one thing in the world that was more powerful than the power of evil, and that was applying its energy to do good. It was also the heart of the message he craved to send to his family in the hereafter: if, in his helplessness, he hadn't prevented their being taken away from him by brute force, he had enough force in him to join them voluntarily. And not just to join them as a volunteer, but as a volunteer whose joining the ranks would make it possible for a commander to emerge. Akiba's father, after all, had always spoken of Moishele as of a future gaon, and he, Akiba, would now enable him to become one!

The very thought, moreover, that the future gaon had been selected for the ovens on account of his physical size, filled Akiba with a furious energy. He had an irresistible desire to disqualify the authority of the wooden Baal to judge a man by going, so to speak, over its head. Wasn't it wonderful for him, Akiba asked himself, to demonstrate with his own life, precisely on the day of Rosh Hashana, when all creatures pass before Him in judgment like sheep, that he cannot pass like a sheep under a wooden idol set up by the Nazis to measure man by his size?

He had always tried to take Moishele as his measure in Torah study. He was, in fact, always jealous of Moishele's assiduity, but it was the creative jealousy of which he had read in the works of the sages of old—the jealousy among the learned which increases wisdom. His reverential jealousy of Moishele was that Rosh Hashana day in Auschwitz immeasurably fortified, if not actually sanctified, by a newly acquired sense of jealousy not just of, but for him. Akiba intuitively grasped the difference: it is one thing to be jealous of someone's achievements, but it is something else to be jealous for one's honor. And the honor involved here was not only Moishele's, but, yes, that of God Himself! The powerful words invoked by the fiery prophet Elijah facing the prophets of Baal came to his mind: "I am jealous for the sake of the Lord God of Hosts."

Of course, Akiba thought, the rabbi had warned him time and again that according to the Torah one's own life comes first, and that nobody but God Himself can determine the value of human life, the merit of human souls. Akiba remembered quite distinctly the talmudic source of the relevant law in Baba Metzia. He had in fact studied it under Moishele a year or so prior to the deportation, when the latter had prepared him for his Bar Mitzvah speech. Two men are traveling on a journey far from human habitations. One of them has a jug of water. If they both drink, they will not have enough to survive. If one drinks, he will live, but his friend will perish. Ben Petura expounded, "Better that both drink and die than that one witness the death of the other." Rabbi Akiba disagreed. "What is meant by the passage in Leviticus 'That thy brother may live with thee' is that in such a case your life takes precedence." Akiba wasn't sure, the rabbi's warning notwithstanding, whether the Law upheld Rabbi Akiba's position. He asked himself, What would the Law be if the companion in question were your teacher? He couldn't fill his place in life, now he would fill his place in death, and not only replace him, but, yes, be him! In the list of the doomed youths a few barracks away, there appeared, of course, Moishele's name. Now Moishele's name, Akiba speculated, just by being replaced with his own—which might not be a replacement at all—could become part of him as a spirit. Dying instead of Moishele and, above all, as Moishele, would put the two of them, as it were, on equal footing.

For a long while, the tall, blond boy with the honest, artless face sat there eyeing the sun in front of him with the intensity of one who responds to a similar intensity confidently eyeing him. A story about the Baal Shem Tov came to his mind. He had heard it from his father in Auschwitz, and it dealt with a transgression that the Baal Shem Tov had committed unwittingly. But because the Almighty is very strict with His chosen—it is written in Psalms, "And His environs are very stormy"—the saintly man was told in a dream that he had forfeited his share in the world to come. The Baal Shem Tov's reaction was one of gratitude: "Now," he exclaimed, "I shall be able to serve my Master just for His own sake alone, without any hope for reward whatsoever."

Akiba was not sure whether this argument could at all be applied in his case. What he did know was that, if a dispute arose before the Supreme Judge about the status of his soul, he would be ready to face it. He had, after all, a few bitter questions of his own to submit to his Maker, questions, he was sure, that if submitted to human judges would make the hair on their heads stand on end in horror. Now, as he was about to rise in the glowing face of a declining sun, he had no questions, but an answer. That answer, he thought, he could give not just with his death, but with his choosing his death. A great passion seized his soul as he rose. "And all living creatures," he quoted rather loudly from the Rosh Hashana prayers he had invoked earlier that day, "pass before Thee like sheep."

"Before Thee," he repeated as he walked toward the quarantined barracks, "not before a man-made measure of man, not before an idol!"

The Kapo, a man with the expressionless, bulbous face of a village commissar on parade, was the one whom Akiba had most feared and loathed in the camp. He was also the one of whom his father had said that to look at his face, as at the faces of the Nazis, was to be defiled. Now, however, he was loath to fear him. He had spoken to him earlier that day, before he first went to the rabbi, and he had told him that he would have both the money and the boy to ransom Moishele. As he came back to him now with the money and the disclosure that he himself was Moishele's substitute, there was some movement in the Kapo's face, which Akiba was now less hesitant to look at. The Kapo now appeared to him as the guardian of a gate leading up to a great and sacred Academy the admissions test to which was indeed very painful, but indispensable for the greater glory of God and His Torah, which one keeps on learning even in the hereafter. The Kapo now bothered him only as would a ferocious dog guarding the entrance to a royal palace: his bite was the entrance ticket.

The Kapo asked Akiba why he was doing this, and Akiba replied that he wouldn't understand. The Kapo asked what Moishele was to him, and Akiba replied, "My teacher." The Kapo asked what he was teaching him, and Akiba said, "Torah."

The small, extinguished eyes in the Kapo's large, bloodless face blinked. "Even with the money and the substitute," he said, "I'm still taking a risk with what I'm doing. Do you know that?"

Akiba did not answer. The Kapo asked Akiba what he wanted him to tell Moishele, and Akiba replied that he could only tell him what not to tell Moishele, namely, that he was going in his stead. When the Kapo said that he would soon find out, anyway. Akiba replied, "But not now, not now!"

A little later, in the stark afterglow of a fiery sunset, Moishele, dazed beyond comprehension, was out of the quarantined barracks. Soon afterward Akiba, taller than any of the sixty youngsters awaiting the end, was standing in their midst with the compelling presence of one meant to be looked up to, though trying to look smaller. His luminous head rose over the petrified faces like the strange glow of an impending sunrise. Did anybody in the group, some of them children, realize that they had a volunteer in their midst? And if anybody did realize it, did it help

soothe the terror in their hearts? We shall never know the
answer. And though we shall never know for sure, I venture to
guess what happened to Moishele. Moishele, I believe, upon
finding out about his replacement, went out of his mind. Or
maybe it was not that Moishele went out of his mind; his mind
went out of Moishele. It went out of him so as to seek reunion
with the soul of Akiba.

Nor was this the first time that the soul of Moshe—of another,
much earlier Moshe, to be sure—was permitted by Him on
High to marvel at the soul of yet another Akiba. As the sages of
the Talmud tell us, in the course of the forty days which Moses
spent face-to-face with the Lord on Mount Sinai, He showed
him, in the luminous mirror of days to come, the image of an
extraordinarily great man, destined to die as a martyr, who more
than anybody else after Moses would further the tradition of
Torah in Israel. His name, as was revealed to Moses by the
Almighty Himself, was Rabbi Akiba.